INKSPIRE

TRAVELS

Revealing Elite Resorts, Hidden Treasures, Authentic Tastes, and Thrilling Adventures for Your Escape

PUNTA CANA Travel Guide 2025

INKSPIRE

Copyright

Disclaimer

The author and publisher have made every effort to ensure the accuracy and completeness of the information contained in this book. However, they assume no responsibility for errors, inaccuracies, omissions, or any other inconsistencies herein. This book is not intended to provide legal, financial, or other professional advice.

About Our Authors

Jeremy Johnson is an acclaimed author in the world of travel writing, celebrated for his vivid and immersive narratives. With a deep curiosity and a gift for storytelling, he brings destinations to life by capturing their true essence and hidden soul. Far more than just a source of tips, his guidebooks inspire mindful exploration and a genuine respect for cultural richness. Whether you're a globe-trotting adventurer or a weekend wanderer, Jeremy's work invites you to travel deeper and connect more meaningfully with the world around you.

Gary Saint is an award-winning travel writer and photographer whose journeys have spanned over 60 countries across six continents during his rich, decade-long career. Known for his vivid storytelling and adventurous spirit, Gary crafts narratives that go far beyond typical travel advice. His work artfully combines useful insights with captivating experiences, all while highlighting his deep admiration for the world's cultures and landscapes. A strong believer in travel as a force for good, Gary's guides encourage readers—from seasoned globetrotters to curious newcomers—to explore with purpose and embrace the wonders of our planet.

SCAN THE QR CODE

- Open your phone's camera app
- Most smartphones have a built-in QR scanner in the camera.
- Point the camera at the QR code
- Make sure the code is clear and within the frame.
- Wait for the notification
- A link or message should pop up on your screen.
- Tap the notification
- This will open the link or content in your browser or a relevant app.
- Follow the instructions on the screen
- You will be taken to a Google Maps, app where you can now click on your current location to get to your destination.

Table of Content

Introduction

The warm Caribbean air hit me like a wave as I stepped off the plane and into the vibrant buzz of Punta Cana. The hum of life here was infectious, as though the entire island was pulsing with energy. It was my first time in this tropical paradise, and every detail was new, exciting, and, frankly, a little overwhelming. As I made my way through the airport, I could feel the excitement building—this was the beginning of a journey I knew would change the way I thought about travel forever.

The first thing that struck me was the vivid color of the sky—an electric blue that seemed to stretch endlessly into the horizon. It was unlike anything I had ever seen. The sun blazed high above, casting its golden light over the lush landscapes and crystal-clear waters. Everything seemed to be in perfect harmony, as if Punta Cana had been waiting for me to discover its secrets.

As I stepped outside the airport, the vibrant sound of merengue music greeted me, filling the air with a rhythmic pulse that felt like the heartbeat of the island. I could smell the salt of the sea and the sweetness of tropical fruits in the breeze. The excitement in the air was contagious, and I could hardly wait to get started on my exploration. I felt like a kid again, eager to uncover the hidden gems of this enchanting place.

Little did I know that what awaited me in Punta Cana was more than just picturesque beaches and luxurious resorts. It was an experience that would immerse me in the local culture, introduce me to unforgettable adventures, and challenge me to slow down and truly savor the moments. From the bustling streets to the tranquil shores, from the culinary delights to the friendly locals, every part of this place offered something new, something exhilarating, something that would make my heart race with wonder.

This book is my story, my journey through Punta Cana in 2025. But it's more than just my adventure—it's a guide that will help you experience the best of this stunning destination. Whether you're seeking pristine beaches, thrilling excursions, or a taste of local culture, this guide will take you through every step of your own unforgettable journey. Welcome to Punta Cana. Let's dive in together.

Welcome to the Punta Cana

It's the sound of the waves that first draws you in. Soft, steady, and comforting, the rhythm of the Caribbean Sea is the heartbeat of Punta Cana. When you close your eyes, it's easy to imagine yourself drifting with it, lulled into a sense of calm that only a place like this can offer. But there's so much more to this stunning Dominican paradise. Punta Cana in 2025 is a vibrant blend of natural beauty, modern attractions, and a rich cultural history, all waiting for you to explore. It's a destination that promises not only an escape from everyday life but an experience that will stay with you long after you've left.

Punta Cana is known for its breathtaking beaches, but it's the hidden corners and the stories of the people here that truly make it stand out. In this guide, I'll take you beyond the sun-soaked shores and the all-inclusive resorts. We'll dive into the heart of this dynamic destination, where adventure, culture, relaxation, and discovery await. But before we get into the nitty-gritty of your journey, let's take a moment to understand why Punta Cana is such a special place to visit in 2025, and how this guide will help you make the most of your time here.

Why Punta Cana in 2025?

Punta Cana has always been a dream destination, but in 2025, there's a certain magic to the place that feels even more alive than before. There's something different in the air—maybe it's the result of the years of careful development or the fresh wave of energy brought on by international events. Whatever it is, Punta Cana's transformation over the years has made it an even more enticing destination for travelers looking to escape the ordinary.

The incredible beaches that once made Punta Cana famous are still as gorgeous as ever, with their powdery white sand and crystal-clear waters. But the resort areas have grown, offering a wider range of accommodations, from ultra-luxurious resorts with private pools to charming boutique hotels that offer a more intimate experience. Punta Cana is not just a place for beach lovers anymore. With the booming eco-tourism scene and an increase in sustainable travel, travelers now have access to a variety of experiences that weren't always available.

The island's natural wonders are a key reason why 2025 is the perfect year to visit. Punta Cana has invested in protecting its rich biodiversity, with new eco-resorts and nature preserves offering opportunities to explore the vibrant jungles and unique wildlife that make the Dominican Republic so special. The rise of adventure tourism is another reason why 2025 is a fantastic time to visit—imagine ziplining through lush canopies, exploring cenotes, or discovering hidden caves that few tourists have had the privilege of seeing.

On top of that, the local culture is thriving, with more emphasis on authentic Dominican experiences. Whether you're visiting a local market, enjoying traditional dishes, or attending a cultural festival, you'll have the chance to connect with the people and the traditions that make Punta Cana more than just a tourist destination.

But perhaps the biggest draw in 2025 is the island's dedication to sustainability and responsible tourism. With eco-friendly initiatives taking center stage, Punta Cana is redefining what it means to travel responsibly while still offering a luxurious experience. From reducing plastic waste to supporting local communities, this new approach makes Punta Cana not only a beautiful place to visit but a place that is committed to making a positive impact on the environment and its people.

Punta Cana is in a constant state of evolution, embracing its growth while staying rooted in its authenticity. In 2025, the destination feels like a perfect blend of old and new, where traditions meet modernity, and where adventure and relaxation coexist seamlessly.

Top Reasons to Visit

There are countless reasons to visit Punta Cana in 2025, and as you begin to plan your journey, these top reasons will surely help guide your decision.

1. Unparalleled Beaches

The beaches in Punta Cana are world-renowned for a reason. Imagine walking along miles of white sand, the Caribbean Sea stretching out before you in every direction. Whether you're looking for a lively stretch of beach with beach bars and activities or a quiet, secluded cove to escape the crowds, you'll find your slice of paradise here. Bavaro Beach, one of the most famous beaches in Punta Cana, is just the beginning. You can also explore the stunning coastline at Macao Beach, a favorite among surfers, or take a boat to the hidden beauty of Saona Island.

2. Luxurious Resorts and All-Inclusive Options

For those who want to relax in style, Punta Cana's world-class resorts are waiting to pamper you. Many of the resorts are all-inclusive, meaning you don't have to lift a finger—everything from meals and drinks to excursions is included in the price of your stay. Whether you choose an upscale beachfront resort or a boutique hotel with a local touch, the variety of accommodations in Punta Cana ensures there's something for every type of traveler. Most resorts offer more than just luxury; they also deliver experiences that connect you with the surrounding environment, like private beach dinners, spa treatments using local ingredients, and immersive cultural activities.

3. Adventure Awaits

If you're the type of traveler who craves adventure, Punta Cana has plenty to offer. From the rugged beauty of the mountains to the mysterious allure of the caves, there's no shortage of thrilling activities. Ziplining through the dense jungles, riding ATVs along rugged trails, and exploring the underwater world with snorkeling and scuba diving are just a few ways to experience Punta Cana's natural wonders. Don't forget the ever-popular dune buggy tours and the opportunity to swim in cenotes—natural sinkholes that reveal some of the most stunning views in the Caribbean.

4. Vibrant Local Culture

While Punta Cana is a popular resort destination, its charm is rooted in its local culture. The island's history is rich with stories of indigenous peoples, African heritage, and colonial influence, all of which have shaped the modern Dominican way of life. In 2025, there is a growing effort to bring visitors closer to this culture through authentic experiences. You can explore traditional Dominican villages, take cooking classes to learn how to make iconic dishes like mangu and sancocho, or attend one of the many lively festivals that celebrate the nation's rich music, art, and dance.

5. Sustainability and Eco-Tourism

More and more, travelers are seeking out destinations that align with their values, and Punta Cana is leading the way in sustainable tourism. From eco-friendly resorts to wildlife protection initiatives, there's a clear commitment to preserving the island's natural beauty for generations to come. You can take part in eco-tours, plant trees, and visit conservation centers that focus on protecting local flora and fauna. This responsible tourism ensures that as Punta Cana grows, it does so in a way that respects both the environment and the local communities.

6. Year-Round Perfect Weather

Punta Cana's tropical climate means it's always a good time to visit. The region enjoys a year-round warm climate with pleasant trade winds that help keep the heat at bay. Whether you're visiting in the winter to escape the cold or planning a summer vacation, the consistent weather makes Punta Cana a reliable destination for sun-seekers. And with temperatures rarely dipping below 75°F (24°C), it's a place that beckons no matter the season.

7. A Strong Focus on Wellness

In 2025, wellness tourism is booming, and Punta Cana has embraced this trend with open arms. The island offers a wide range of wellness-focused resorts and activities, from yoga and meditation on the beach to spa retreats that use local, organic ingredients. Many of the resorts are designed with relaxation in mind, offering wellness packages that include massages, detox programs, and fitness classes. Whether you want to unwind after a busy day of adventure or simply relax and rejuvenate,

Punta Cana's wellness offerings will help you do just that.

How to Use This Guide

Now that you know why Punta Cana is such an enticing destination in 2025, it's time to dive into the details. This guide is designed to be your companion throughout your journey, helping you navigate everything from where to stay to what to eat, and everything in between. But the key to getting the most out of this book is to approach it with flexibility. Everyone's trip to Punta Cana is unique, and while this guide provides plenty of suggestions and recommendations, it's meant to be a jumping-off point for your own personalized adventure.

Here's how to get the most out of this guide:

1. Read Ahead, But Stay Flexible

Punta Cana is full of surprises. While it's helpful to plan ahead, you'll want to leave room for spontaneity. As you read through each section, highlight the places that intrigue you, but don't be afraid to change course once you're here. Sometimes the best experiences come from following your instincts, whether it's taking a detour to a hidden beach or discovering a local gem that wasn't in the guidebook.

2. Use the Itineraries to Plan Your Trip

The sample itineraries provided will give you a solid foundation for planning your stay. Whether you have three days or seven, these itineraries are designed to help you experience the best of Punta Cana, no matter how much time you have. But remember, these are just starting points. You can adjust them based on your interests and the pace at which you want to travel.

3. Immerse Yourself in Local Culture

As much as Punta Cana is a place for relaxation and luxury, it's also a place to connect with the people who call it home. This guide emphasizes the importance of exploring beyond the resort walls and engaging with the island's rich cultural heritage. Seek out local markets, try traditional foods, and talk to the friendly residents who can offer insights into the area that you won't find in any guidebook.

4. Keep Sustainability in Mind

Punta Cana is working hard to protect its natural beauty, and so should you. This guide includes tips on responsible tourism, from eco-friendly excursions to minimizing your environmental footprint. By following these suggestions, you'll be supporting the island's commitment to sustainability and helping preserve Punta Cana's magic for future generations.

When to Visit Punta Cana

Punta Cana, with its tropical climate and stunning landscapes, is an attractive destination year-round. But when is the absolute best time to visit? Depending on what you want out of your experience, the ideal time to visit this Caribbean paradise can vary. Whether you're planning a family vacation, a romantic getaway, or an adventure-filled trip, the timing can make all the difference in ensuring your Punta Cana experience is as memorable as possible.

In this section, we'll break down the various seasons in Punta Cana, offer a month-by-month breakdown of weather conditions, events, and pricing, and help you decide when the best time to go really is. Let's dive in!

Peak vs. Off-Peak Seasons: What to Know

When planning a trip to Punta Cana, one of the most important things to consider is the season. Punta Cana experiences two major seasons: the peak season (high season) and the off-peak season (low season). Each season comes with its own set of advantages and drawbacks, and understanding these differences will help you plan accordingly.

Peak Season (High Season)

The peak season in Punta Cana typically runs from December to April. During this time, the weather is at its most pleasant—hot, sunny days and clear skies, with minimal rainfall. This makes it the perfect time to visit for beach lovers, sun-seekers, and those looking for ideal conditions for outdoor activities. However, because of the favorable weather, the island sees a significant increase in tourists, and prices tend to be higher.

Airfares, hotel rates, and tour prices all peak during the high season, which means you'll need to book early if you want to secure the best deals. Although the crowds can be large, especially around the holidays (Christmas, New Year's, and Easter), the lively atmosphere, special events, and festive vibe make it an exciting time to visit.

This is also when many of the luxurious resorts, high-end hotels, and exclusive experiences are at their best, offering the best service and amenities. But it's important to note that because of the higher demand, reservations for popular activities and excursions can fill up fast. So, if you're visiting during this time, it's best to plan ahead and book your activities well in advance.

Off-Peak Season (Low Season)

The off-peak season in Punta Cana runs from May to November, and it comes with a different set of advantages. During this period, the weather can be a bit more unpredictable, with more frequent rain showers and higher humidity. However, temperatures still remain warm, and while it's not as consistently sunny as the high season, it can still be a great time to visit.

The major advantage of visiting Punta Cana during the off-peak season is the reduced number of tourists. The beaches are less crowded, and you can often find great deals on hotels, flights, and excursions. This is especially true if you're flexible with your travel dates. You'll also enjoy more personalized attention at resorts and attractions, as there are fewer visitors overall.

Another key consideration for the off-peak season is the hurricane season, which runs from June to November. While the risk of a hurricane directly affecting Punta Cana is low, it's still something to keep in mind when planning your trip. That said, if you take the proper precautions and are willing to be flexible with your travel dates, visiting during this season can offer the best value for money.

Month-by-Month Breakdown: Weather, Events, and Pricing

Each month in Punta Cana offers a slightly different experience, depending on the weather, local events, and pricing. Below, I'll walk you through a month-by-month breakdown of what you can expect.

December – February

These months are considered the peak of the high season. Temperatures range from the low 70s to mid-80s (°F), with minimal rainfall and plenty of sunshine. This is when Punta Cana is at its most vibrant, with large crowds of tourists flocking to the beaches for the holidays. Prices are at their highest during these months, especially during Christmas and New Year's. If you're looking for a lively atmosphere, plenty of events, and no shortage of sunshine, this is the time to be here. Just be prepared to book early and pay a premium for accommodations and activities.

March – April

March and April continue the high season trend, although by April, the crowds start to thin out a bit, especially after spring break. The weather remains warm and sunny, with average temperatures in the low 80s (°F). This is a great time to visit if you prefer to avoid the holiday rush but still want the perfect weather for outdoor activities. Prices begin to drop in late April, making it a good time to visit if you want to balance good weather with a more manageable price tag.

May

May marks the beginning of the off-peak season, and while the weather is still warm, it does tend to get hotter and more humid. Average temperatures hover around the mid-80s (°F), with occasional afternoon showers. Prices drop significantly compared to the high season, making it a great time for budget-conscious travelers. The crowds are thinner, and you'll have a more relaxed and quiet experience on the beach. It's still a good time to enjoy the sunshine without the hustle and bustle of peak season.

June – August

June through August are the hottest months in Punta Cana, with temperatures in the upper 80s to low 90s (°F) during the day. It's also the start of hurricane season, so expect higher humidity and more rain. However, you can still expect plenty of sunny days, and the resorts offer enticing deals to attract visitors during the quieter months. The upside of visiting during these months is that you'll get much lower prices compared to the high season, and the beaches are far less crowded. If you don't mind the heat and the occasional rain shower, this can be a fantastic time to visit.

September – October

September and October are the wettest months in Punta Cana, with higher chances of rainfall and tropical storms. This is also when the risk of hurricanes is higher, although Punta Cana is often spared from direct hits. Temperatures remain hot, but the increased rain and humidity can make it uncomfortable for some travelers. That said, if you're looking for low prices and don't mind the weather risks, this is the most budget-friendly time to visit. Crowds are sparse, and many resorts offer fantastic discounts during these months.

November

By November, the weather begins to improve as the rainy season winds down. Temperatures are still warm, but the humidity starts to drop, making it more comfortable for outdoor activities. The crowds are still relatively low, and prices start to rise slightly as the high season approaches. November can be an excellent time to visit if you want to avoid the worst of the rain but still enjoy affordable prices and fewer tourists.

High Season, Low Season, and Hidden Deals

Navigating between high and low season can be tricky, but knowing when to book can make a huge difference in your experience and budget.

High Season Deals

While high season is synonymous with higher prices, there are still some ways to find deals. Many resorts offer promotions such as early bird discounts, packages, and special offers that can make the high season a bit more affordable. Booking well in advance is key if you want to lock in the best deals during this time.

Low Season Deals

Low season is where Punta Cana truly shines for budget-conscious travelers. While you'll sacrifice some of the perfect weather, the lower prices, fewer crowds, and more intimate experiences can more than make up for it. During these months, last-minute deals and package discounts are abundant, so if you have the flexibility, you can score amazing deals on flights and resorts.

Hidden Deals

For those willing to take a chance, there are always hidden gems during the shoulder months (like November and late April). If you can manage to travel during the transitions between high and low season, you can enjoy the benefits of both worlds: great weather, lower prices, and fewer tourists. Keep an eye out for special offers and packages that combine flights and hotels for the best value.

Best Times for Family, Romantic, and Adventure Trips

Different types of travelers will have different preferences when it comes to timing their Punta Cana getaway. Here's a breakdown of the best times for various types of trips:

Family Trips

The best time to visit Punta Cana for a family vacation is during the high season, particularly in March and April, when the weather is ideal for outdoor activities and the schools are on break. The resorts here cater to families, offering kid-friendly activities, clubs, and entertainment. If you prefer fewer crowds and more affordable options, May and November are also great months for family trips.

Romantic Getaways

For couples seeking romance and intimacy, the ideal time to visit Punta Cana is during the low season. Fewer tourists mean more peaceful beaches, quieter resorts, and a more relaxed atmosphere. September and October are perfect for those who want a secluded getaway, but if you prefer guaranteed sunny days, March through April offers great weather with fewer tourists than the peak months.

Adventure Trips

Adventure seekers will love Punta Cana year-round, but the best time to visit for an action-packed trip is during the dry months of the high season, from December to April. The weather will be perfect for zip-lining, hiking, and exploring the surrounding nature. If you're not a fan of large crowds, opt for the shoulder months like May or November for a more adventurous but less crowded experience.

Where to Stay in Punta Cana

Punta Cana is known for its stunning beaches, vibrant culture, and world-class resorts, making it a popular destination for travelers seeking relaxation, adventure, and everything in between. Whether you're looking for the ultimate luxury experience, a cozy boutique stay, or a hidden gem off the beaten path, Punta Cana offers a variety of accommodations to suit every style, preference, and budget.

In this section, we'll dive into the best areas to stay in Punta Cana, comparing all-inclusive resorts with boutique hotels, and offering recommendations for luxury properties, eco-friendly lodges, and more affordable options. We'll also share some lesser-known, hidden gems that will make your trip even more memorable. Let's start exploring where to lay your head while enjoying everything Punta Cana has to offer.

Top Resort Areas: Bávaro, Cap Cana, Uvero Alto, Macao

Punta Cana is home to several key resort areas, each offering its unique appeal. When choosing where to stay, understanding the vibe and amenities of each neighborhood will help you find the perfect spot for your getaway.

Bávaro: The Heart of Punta Cana's Tourism Scene

Bávaro is arguably the most popular area in Punta Cana, and for good reason. Located just 30 minutes from the airport, Bávaro is home to some of the most luxurious all-inclusive resorts, pristine beaches, and a vibrant nightlife scene. This area is perfect for visitors who want to be at the center of the action, with easy access to beach clubs, restaurants, and local shops.

The beaches in Bávaro are some of the most beautiful in the Dominican Republic, with powdery white sand and turquoise waters. Many resorts in Bávaro offer all-inclusive packages, which make it easy to indulge in gourmet dining, spa treatments, and activities without leaving the property. This area is perfect for families, couples, and groups seeking convenience, luxury, and a wide range of entertainment options.

Cap Cana: Exclusive Luxury and Tranquil Vibes

If you're seeking an upscale, tranquil retreat, Cap Cana is the place to be. Located just 20 minutes from the Punta Cana airport, Cap Cana is a high-end resort community known for its luxurious resorts, world-class golf courses, and beautiful beaches. It's a quieter, more exclusive area compared to Bávaro, attracting travelers looking for privacy, relaxation, and sophistication.

The resorts in Cap Cana are often more intimate and less crowded, offering an elevated experience with stunning views and exceptional service. Many of the hotels here cater to adults and couples, offering the perfect setting for romantic getaways or peaceful escapes. If you enjoy golfing, Cap Cana is home to one of the best courses in the Caribbean, Punta Espada Golf Course, which has breathtaking ocean views. Cap Cana is also home to some of the best beach clubs and private villas, making it the ideal destination for those seeking both luxury and serenity.

Uvero Alto: Secluded Paradise and Authentic Vibes

Located to the north of Bávaro, Uvero Alto is a quieter, more laid-back resort area perfect for those who want to escape the crowds and enjoy a more relaxed vibe. While it's still close enough to enjoy the attractions and nightlife of Bávaro, Uvero Alto offers a more secluded and peaceful atmosphere, making it ideal for couples and families who want to unwind in a more intimate setting.

Many of the all-inclusive resorts in Uvero Alto are set within lush tropical surroundings, providing a sense of being immersed in nature. The beaches here are beautiful, less crowded, and perfect for those who want to enjoy a more tranquil beach experience. Uvero Alto is also home to some fantastic boutique hotels and resorts that focus on personalized service, providing a more intimate and exclusive feel.

Macao: Hidden Gem for Surfers and Nature Lovers

Macao, located to the north of Uvero Alto, is a hidden gem for those seeking a more adventurous and off-the-beaten-path experience. Known for its surf-friendly beaches and rugged natural beauty, Macao offers a more rustic, authentic feel compared to the more polished resort areas. It's a great choice for those who want to experience the natural beauty of the Dominican Republic without the crowds.

The beach here is less developed and often frequented by local surfers and nature enthusiasts.

If you're interested in water sports, Macao is one of the best places to try surfing or simply enjoy the raw beauty of the coastline. While accommodations in Macao are more limited, there are still a few boutique hotels and eco-friendly lodges that offer a unique and intimate stay, allowing you to connect with nature and the local culture.

Comparing All-Inclusive vs. Boutique Stays

Punta Cana is famous for its all-inclusive resorts, but if you're not a fan of large resorts and prefer something more intimate, boutique hotels offer an excellent alternative. Let's take a closer look at the pros and cons of both types of accommodations.

All-Inclusive Resorts: Convenience and Luxury

All-inclusive resorts are the cornerstone of Punta Cana's hospitality scene. These resorts offer the ultimate in convenience, as they typically include meals, drinks, activities, and entertainment all in one price. For many travelers, especially those traveling with families or groups, the all-inclusive model is a great way to relax and not worry about additional costs.

The large all-inclusive resorts in Punta Cana are often packed with amenities, from expansive pools and spas to beach clubs and water sports. They also offer a variety of dining options, with gourmet restaurants, buffets, and bars available throughout the property. For families, these resorts often have kids' clubs, water parks, and entertainment options that will keep younger travelers entertained.

However, the downside to all-inclusive resorts is that they can be crowded and somewhat impersonal. The focus is often on mass tourism, which can result in less attention to individual preferences. Additionally, while you have access to everything on the property, you may miss out on the local culture and dining experiences outside of the resort.

Boutique Hotels: Intimate Charm and Local Flavors

Boutique hotels, on the other hand, offer a more personalized experience. These smaller properties focus on providing unique accommodations, exceptional service, and a connection to local culture. If you're seeking a more intimate stay, boutique hotels in Punta Cana provide an opportunity to experience the island in a different way, with local influences, carefully curated decor, and a focus on authenticity.

Many boutique hotels are located in less touristy areas, allowing you to experience the authentic side of Punta Cana. Some offer a more eco-conscious approach, with sustainable practices and designs that reflect the natural beauty of the area. You'll also find more opportunities to sample local cuisine at boutique hotels, where chefs often focus on using fresh, local ingredients to create delicious dishes.

The downside to boutique hotels is that they may not offer the same level of amenities as all-inclusive resorts. However, the trade-off is that you'll get a more intimate and authentic experience, with fewer crowds and more attention to detail.

Best Luxury Resorts, Eco-Friendly Lodges, and Affordable Options

Whether you're looking to splurge on a luxury resort, stay in an eco-friendly lodge, or find an affordable option that still offers comfort and charm, Punta Cana has accommodations for every budget.

Luxury Resorts: The Pinnacle of Elegance and Comfort

For those looking to indulge in the ultimate luxury experience, Punta Cana has a number of high-end resorts that offer everything you could ever need and more. From private villas and oceanfront suites to fine dining and exclusive activities, luxury resorts in Punta Cana are designed to offer an unforgettable experience.

Some of the best luxury resorts include the **Eden Roc at Cap Cana**, a Relais & Châteaux property, which offers exclusive villas with private pools, an award-winning restaurant, and a spa. **The Sanctuary Cap Cana** is another top choice, known for its adults-only atmosphere and spacious suites with ocean views.

Eden Roc at Cap Cana

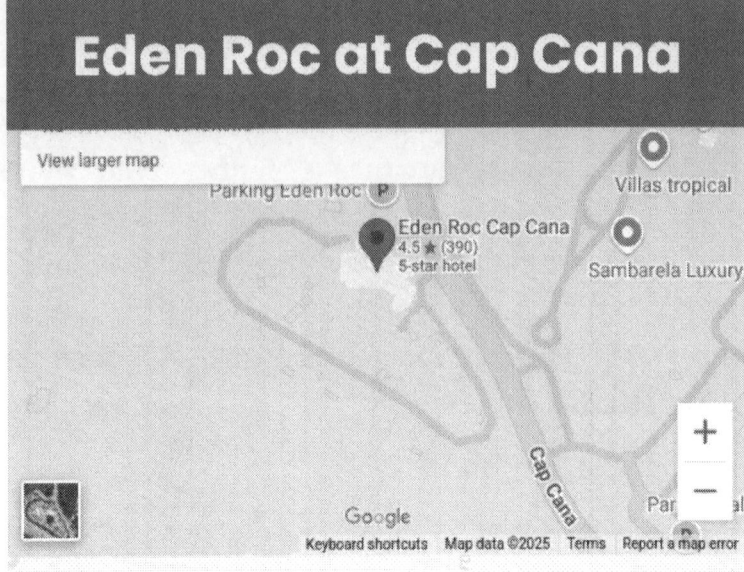

SCAN THE QR CODE

- Open your phone's camera app
- Most smartphones have a built-in QR scanner in the camera.
- Point the camera at the QR code
- Make sure the code is clear and within the frame.
- Wait for the notification
- A link or message should pop up on your screen.
- Tap the notification
- This will open the link or content in your browser or a relevant app.
- Follow the instructions on the screen
- You will be taken to a Google Maps, app where you can now click on your current location to get to your destination.

Eco-Friendly Lodges: Sustainable Stays with a Conscience

If sustainability is a priority for you, there are several eco-friendly lodges and resorts in Punta Cana that offer an environmentally conscious experience. The **Puntacana Resort & Club**, for example, is dedicated to preserving the natural environment and supporting local communities. The property features sustainable design, conservation efforts, and offers guests the chance to experience the beauty of Punta Cana in an eco-friendly way.

Additionally, the **Indigenous Beach Resort** is a unique eco-resort that promotes sustainability while offering an immersive nature experience. Staying at eco-lodges not only supports sustainable tourism but also allows you to enjoy Punta Cana's natural beauty in a meaningful way.

Affordable Options: Comfort Without Breaking the Bank

Punta Cana also has plenty of affordable hotels and resorts that offer excellent value for money. While they may not have all the bells and whistles of a luxury resort, they provide comfortable accommodations and easy access to the island's best attractions. Consider staying at **The Ocean Blue & Sand Resort**, which offers an all-inclusive package at a more affordable price point, or **Bávaro Beach Hotel**, a budget-friendly option with a great location and excellent service.

Hidden Hotel Gems You Won't Find in Other Guides

If you're the type of traveler who wants to discover something off the beaten path, Punta Cana is home to a few hidden gems that most tourists don't know about. One of these gems is the **Hotel Flor de Mar**, a small boutique hotel that offers personalized service and is located just steps from the beach. Another hidden gem is **Casa de Campo Resort**, an exclusive property offering world-class amenities but without the usual crowds.

These lesser-known properties offer the chance to stay in smaller, more intimate settings, allowing you to experience Punta Cana in a way that feels more personal and unique.

Beaches of Punta Cana

When it comes to tropical escapes, few places rival the allure of Punta Cana's pristine beaches. Known for its powdery white sands and crystal-clear waters, Punta Cana's coastline stretches for miles, offering a variety of beach experiences that cater to every type of traveler. Whether you're here to bask in the sun, try your hand at water sports, or explore hidden, tranquil coves, this guide will help you discover the very best Punta Cana has to offer when it comes to its beaches.

In this section, we'll take you on a journey to the best beaches in Punta Cana for swimming, sunbathing, and water sports. We'll also uncover some secret spots that are perfect for those seeking a peaceful getaway, dive into the most Instagrammable beaches and scenic spots, and share beach etiquette tips to ensure you have an enjoyable experience while respecting local customs. So grab your sunscreen and get ready for an unforgettable beach adventure.

Punta Cana's Best Beaches for Swimming, Sunbathing, and Water Sports

Punta Cana is home to some of the most beautiful beaches in the Caribbean, each with its own unique characteristics. Whether you're a seasoned swimmer, a sunbather, or a water sports enthusiast, you'll find the perfect spot to suit your needs.

Bávaro Beach: A Tropical Paradise for Swimming and Relaxation

Bávaro Beach is one of the most iconic and well-known beaches in Punta Cana, and for good reason. Stretching for miles along the coastline, it's a stunning blend of soft white sand, turquoise waters, and gentle waves. This beach is perfect for swimming, as the waters here are calm and clear, making it ideal for families, couples, and solo travelers alike.

Bávaro Beach is also home to numerous beachfront resorts, so you'll find plenty of opportunities for sunbathing and enjoying the natural beauty of the area. While it can get busy at times, the wide expanse of beach ensures that you can always find a quiet spot to unwind. If you're into water sports, Bávaro offers an array of activities, from jet skiing and parasailing to windsurfing and snorkeling. The beach is a hub of activity, so whether you're relaxing under a palm tree or gearing up for an adventure on the water, Bávaro Beach has something for everyone.

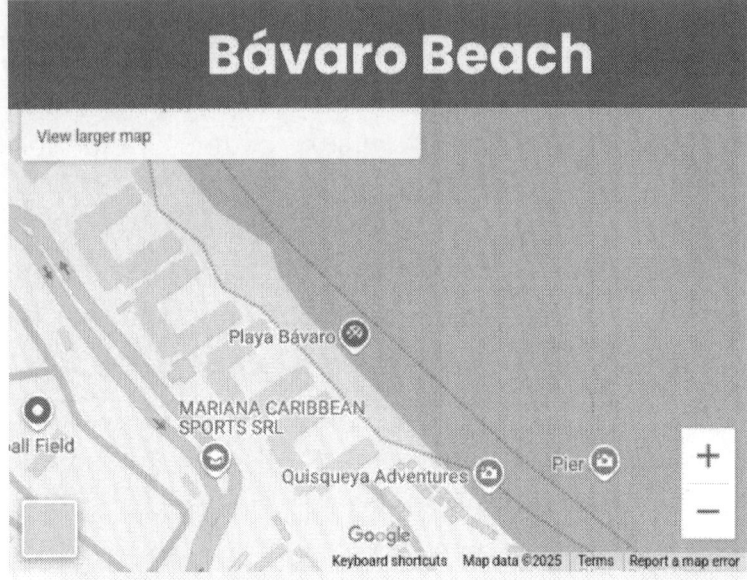

Bávaro Beach

View larger map

SCAN THE QR CODE

- Open your phone's camera app
- Most smartphones have a built-in QR scanner in the camera.
- Point the camera at the QR code
- Make sure the code is clear and within the frame.
- Wait for the notification
- A link or message should pop up on your screen.
- Tap the notification
- This will open the link or content in your browser or a relevant app.
- Follow the instructions on the screen
- You will be taken to a Google Maps, app where you can now click on your current location to get to your destination.

Macao Beach: Surfer's Paradise and Tranquil Escape

If you're seeking a quieter beach that still offers plenty of opportunities for adventure, Macao Beach is the place to be. Located about 30 minutes north of Bávaro, Macao is known for its powerful waves and is a popular spot for surfers. The beach itself is less developed than others in Punta Cana, which gives it a more natural and rugged feel.

For those who prefer swimming or sunbathing, Macao Beach still offers plenty of space to relax. The stunning cliffs surrounding the beach and the golden sand make it a perfect place to enjoy the sun while taking in breathtaking views. The waves can be a bit stronger here, so if you're into water sports, Macao is the perfect location to try surfing or bodyboarding. The beach is also less crowded than Bávaro, which means you'll have a more peaceful experience. Macao Beach is ideal for those looking to escape the more tourist-heavy areas and enjoy a quiet day in nature.

Cap Cana's Juanillo Beach: Luxury, Calm Waters, and Excellent Swimming

For those seeking a more exclusive beach experience, Juanillo Beach in Cap Cana offers an idyllic escape. Known for its pristine white sands and crystal-clear waters, this beach is perfect for swimming, relaxing, and enjoying the quiet luxury of the area. Juanillo Beach is surrounded by high-end resorts and private villas, giving it a serene and upscale atmosphere.

The shallow waters here make it ideal for swimming, and the beach is less crowded than Bávaro, which adds to its charm. Whether you're lounging under the palm trees with a cold drink or taking a leisurely swim in the warm waters, Juanillo Beach is a slice of paradise. For those interested in water sports, the calm waters make it an excellent place for stand-up paddleboarding, kayaking, and sailing. It's also one of the best spots in Punta Cana to enjoy a beach picnic, making it a great choice for families and couples.

Secret, Quiet Beaches Away from the Crowds

While Punta Cana is home to several well-known beaches, there are also hidden gems that offer a more secluded and peaceful atmosphere. If you're looking to escape the crowds and experience a quieter side of Punta Cana, here are some lesser-known beaches worth visiting.

El Cortecito Beach: A Local Favorite for Quiet Relaxation

Located between Bávaro and Uvero Alto, El Cortecito Beach is a small, charming beach that is loved by locals and offers a more laid-back atmosphere compared to the larger tourist areas. It's the perfect spot to relax and enjoy the natural beauty of the Dominican Republic. The beach is often less crowded, making it a peaceful escape where you can sunbathe, swim, or just listen to the sound of the waves.

El Cortecito Beach is also a great place to enjoy fresh seafood, with several local beachfront restaurants offering authentic Dominican dishes. The calm waters here are ideal for swimming, and there's a small reef that's perfect for snorkeling. If you're looking for a more authentic and less touristy beach experience, El Cortecito is a hidden gem you won't want to miss.

Blau Punta Cana Beach: A Quiet Retreat for Nature Lovers

Blau Punta Cana Beach, located near the Blau Punta Cana Resort, is another quiet retreat that offers a more peaceful experience compared to the busy resort areas. This beach is often less crowded, making it perfect for those looking for a serene escape. The crystal-clear waters and soft sand make it a great spot to unwind, while the surrounding natural beauty adds to its tranquil atmosphere.

This beach is also close to the **Los Haitises National Park**, a stunning protected area known for its lush mangrove forests, caves, and diverse wildlife. If you're looking for a more remote and peaceful beach experience, Blau Punta Cana Beach is a hidden treasure that's perfect for nature lovers.

The Most Instagrammable Beaches and Spots

Punta Cana is filled with jaw-dropping beaches and scenic spots that are perfect for capturing your vacation moments. From the sparkling blue waters to the lush palm trees, here are some of the most Instagrammable beaches and spots in Punta Cana that will make your followers envious.

Bávaro Beach: Picture-Perfect Paradise

Bávaro Beach is not only one of the best beaches for swimming and sunbathing but also one of the most photogenic locations in Punta Cana. The clear turquoise waters, soft white sand, and swaying palm trees create a postcard-perfect scene that is perfect for your Instagram feed. Whether you're snapping photos of the beach at sunrise, capturing the beauty of the ocean, or posing in front of one of the many beach clubs, Bávaro Beach offers endless photo opportunities.

For a more unique shot, try capturing the reflection of the sky and palm trees in the shallow waters near the shore. It's an iconic image that perfectly captures the beauty of Punta Cana.

Cap Cana's Juanillo Beach: A Luxury Paradise

Juanillo Beach in Cap Cana offers a stunning combination of white sand, calm waters, and luxury resorts, making it one of the most Instagram-worthy spots in Punta Cana. The pristine beach provides the perfect backdrop for stunning photos of the ocean and the beautiful surroundings.

Capture the perfect shot of the beach at sunset, when the golden light bathes the sand and water in a warm glow. Whether you're enjoying a drink at one of the beachfront restaurants or lounging under a cabana, Juanillo Beach offers a chic and sophisticated setting for your vacation photos.

Macau Beach: Surfer's Heaven and Scenic Beauty

Macau Beach is not just known for its surfing opportunities but also for its rugged, untouched beauty. The dramatic cliffs, golden sand, and powerful waves create a stunning contrast, making it one of the most Instagrammable beaches in Punta Cana. Whether you're snapping a photo of the waves crashing against the shore or catching the sunset behind the cliffs, Macau Beach provides a dramatic backdrop for photos that will stand out on your feed.

Beach Etiquette and Local Tips

While enjoying Punta Cana's beautiful beaches, it's important to respect local customs and etiquette. Here are a few tips to ensure you have a fun and respectful beach experience:

- **Respect the Environment:** Always dispose of trash properly and avoid leaving plastic waste behind. Punta Cana's natural beauty is one of its biggest attractions, so it's important to do your part in keeping the beaches clean.

- **Respect Local Culture:** When visiting public beaches, avoid disturbing the local wildlife and be mindful of the local community. If you're staying at a resort, make sure to follow their rules and guidelines for using the beach.

- **Sun Protection:** The sun in Punta Cana can be intense, so make sure to wear sunscreen and protect yourself from overexposure. Consider wearing a hat, sunglasses, and lightweight clothing to stay cool while enjoying the beach.

Whether you're looking to relax on the sand, try water sports, or find the perfect beach for photos,

Punta Cana's beaches have something for everyone. From the iconic Bávaro Beach to hidden gems like Macao and El Cortecito, you'll find a range of experiences that will make your trip unforgettable. So grab your towel, your camera, and your sense of adventure, and let the beautiful beaches of Punta Cana take your breath away.

Things to Do in Punta Cana

When most people think of Punta Cana, images of palm-lined beaches, luxurious resorts, and endless relaxation come to mind. However, there's so much more to this tropical paradise than just sunbathing. Punta Cana offers an exciting mix of adventure, culture, and natural beauty that can turn your vacation into a thrilling, immersive experience. From iconic excursions to hidden gems, the possibilities for adventure and exploration are endless.

In this section, we'll guide you through the top activities and experiences that you can't miss while in Punta Cana. Whether you're seeking adrenaline-pumping activities, a chance to immerse yourself in local culture, or hidden treasures off the beaten path, Punta Cana has something for everyone. So buckle up as we take you on a tour of the must-do activities in this stunning destination.

Iconic Excursions You Can't Miss (Saona Island, Hoyo Azul, etc.)

Punta Cana is home to some of the most iconic excursions that showcase the natural beauty and cultural richness of the Dominican Republic. These excursions are not just activities; they're experiences that you'll carry with you long after you've left.

Saona Island: A Caribbean Dream Come True

One of the most famous and highly recommended excursions in Punta Cana is a day trip to Saona Island. Located off the southeast coast of the Dominican Republic, this island is a part of the East National Park, a protected area that boasts stunning beaches, crystal-clear waters, and vibrant marine life. Saona Island is often described as paradise on earth, and once you set foot on its shores, you'll understand why.

The excursion to Saona Island typically involves a boat ride, often accompanied by a lively party atmosphere. On the way to the island, you'll pass by natural pools in the middle of the ocean, where you can take a refreshing dip in the shallow waters and admire the starfish that dot the sea floor. Upon reaching Saona Island, you'll have time to relax on the beach, enjoy a traditional Dominican lunch, and explore the island's stunning coastline.

For nature lovers, Saona is also an excellent spot for snorkeling. The coral reefs surrounding the island are teeming with marine life, making it a fantastic opportunity to see tropical fish, sea turtles, and colorful corals up close.

Hoyo Azul: A Hidden Gem of Turquoise Waters

If you're seeking a more tranquil and off-the-beaten-path excursion, look no further than Hoyo Azul, a hidden cenote located in the Scape Park at Cap Cana. The name "Hoyo Azul" translates to "Blue Hole," and it's easy to see why. The cenote's waters are a striking shade of turquoise that seems almost unreal.

The journey to Hoyo Azul involves a short hike through the jungle, where you'll pass by lush greenery, rocky terrain, and the occasional glimpse of wildlife. The hike is not overly strenuous, making it suitable for most fitness levels, and the reward at the end is more than worth it. After reaching the cenote, you can take a refreshing swim in the cool, crystal-clear waters surrounded by towering cliffs.

Aside from its natural beauty, Hoyo Azul is a peaceful escape from the bustling resorts and beaches of Punta Cana, offering a more serene and intimate experience. It's a perfect spot for nature lovers and those looking to unwind in a secluded environment.

Thrilling Adventures: Ziplining, Water Sports, and More

For those seeking an adrenaline rush, Punta Cana is packed with exciting activities that will get your heart racing. Whether you're flying through the treetops or riding the waves, the adventure options here are endless.

Ziplining: Soar Above the Jungle

One of the most thrilling ways to experience the natural beauty of Punta Cana is by going ziplining. Several ziplining tours are available, offering you the chance to fly through the treetops of the Dominican Republic's lush rainforests. The zipline courses typically include a series of platforms and cables that take you soaring over rivers, valleys, and jungle canopies, providing spectacular views of the surrounding landscape.

One popular ziplining spot is the Scape Park at Cap Cana, where you can zip across multiple lines, some of which are incredibly long and fast. The experience of gliding through the air while surrounded by the lush green jungle below is exhilarating, making it a must-do activity for adventure lovers.

Water Sports: Dive Into Adventure

Punta Cana's crystal-clear waters make it a prime location for all sorts of water sports. From thrilling activities like jet skiing to more laid-back experiences like paddleboarding, the options are plentiful. Whether you're an experienced water sports enthusiast or a beginner looking to try something new, there's something for everyone.

One popular water activity is parasailing, which allows you to soar high above the ocean and take in panoramic views of the coastline. It's an exhilarating way to experience Punta Cana's beaches from a completely different perspective.

If you're a fan of snorkeling or scuba diving, Punta Cana has several excellent spots where you can explore vibrant coral reefs and encounter marine life like tropical fish, sea turtles, and stingrays. One of the best places for snorkeling is the reef at

Cabeza de Toro, where the calm waters make it an ideal location for underwater exploration.

For those who love kayaking or paddleboarding, the calm waters of Bávaro Beach and Cap Cana are perfect for these activities. You can paddle along the coastline, enjoy the scenery, and even spot some marine life as you glide through the water.

Horseback Riding: Gallop Through Paradise

If you're looking for a more relaxed way to explore the Punta Cana countryside, horseback riding is an excellent option. Several tours are available that take you through the scenic landscapes of the Dominican Republic, including lush forests, rolling hills, and coastal areas. Riding a horse along the beach at sunset is a particularly magical experience, offering a unique perspective of Punta Cana's natural beauty.

Exploring Local Culture: Art, Music, and Traditions

Punta Cana isn't just about beaches and water sports; it's also a place rich in culture and tradition. While you're here, take the time to immerse yourself in the local culture, whether it's through art, music, or cuisine.

Art and Craft Markets: A Glimpse into Dominican Creativity

One of the best ways to experience the culture of the Dominican Republic is through its art and crafts. Punta Cana is home to several artisan markets where you can browse handmade goods, including colorful textiles, pottery, jewelry, and paintings. These markets are perfect for picking up unique souvenirs and gifts while supporting local artists.

The **Bavaro Artisan Village** is one of the most popular spots for art lovers. It's a vibrant market where you can watch artisans at work, creating everything from wood carvings to hand-painted ceramics. It's a great place to learn more about Dominican craftsmanship and take home a piece of the island's culture.

Live Music and Traditional Dance: A Celebration of Dominican Heritage

No trip to Punta Cana would be complete without experiencing the lively music and dance that are such an integral part of Dominican culture.

Merengue and Bachata are the two most popular styles of music in the Dominican Republic, and you'll find plenty of opportunities to enjoy live performances during your visit.

For an authentic experience, attend a **Bachata or Merengue show** at one of the local venues, where talented musicians and dancers will immerse you in the rhythm and energy of the Dominican Republic. If you're feeling adventurous, join in the dancing and learn the steps yourself – there's no better way to embrace the vibrant culture of Punta Cana.

Hidden Treasures: Off-the-Beaten-Path Experiences

While Punta Cana's popular attractions are certainly worth visiting, there are also plenty of hidden treasures waiting to be discovered by those who venture off the beaten path. These experiences offer a more authentic and intimate look at the Dominican Republic.

Los Haitises National Park: Explore the Unspoiled Wilderness

For nature lovers, a trip to **Los Haitises National Park** is a must. Located just a short boat ride from Punta Cana, this protected area is known for its lush mangrove forests, limestone caves, and diverse wildlife. The park is a paradise for birdwatchers, as it's home to over 200 species of birds, including the endangered Hispaniolan parrot.

A boat tour through the park will take you past stunning rock formations, hidden caves, and uninhabited islands. The natural beauty and tranquility of the park make it one of the most off-the-radar yet spectacular experiences in Punta Cana.

Altos de Chavón: A Mediterranean Village in the Caribbean

Another hidden gem is **Altos de Chavón**, a charming replica of a Mediterranean village located high on a hill overlooking the Chavón River. This beautiful and artistic village is home to cobblestone streets, artisan shops, art galleries, and a stunning amphitheater that hosts concerts and performances.

Altos de Chavón is a perfect place to spend an afternoon wandering through its picturesque streets, admiring the local art, and taking in the incredible views. It's a peaceful retreat from the hustle and bustle of the beaches and resorts.

Punta Cana is a destination that offers much more than just beautiful beaches. Whether you're looking for thrilling adventures, cultural experiences, or hidden treasures, the possibilities for exploration are endless. The activities and experiences in this tropical paradise will ensure that your trip is filled with unforgettable memories and stories to share for years to come.

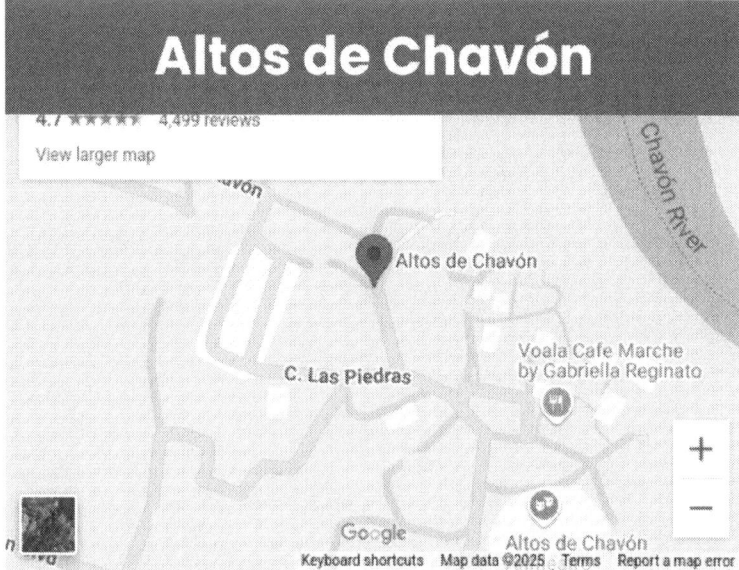

Altos de Chavón

4.7 ★★★★★ 4,499 reviews

View larger map

Altos de Chavón

C. Las Piedras

Voala Cafe Marche
by Gabriella Reginato

Altos de Chavón

Google

Keyboard shortcuts   Map data ©2025   Terms   Report a map error

SCAN THE QR CODE

- Open your phone's camera app
- Most smartphones have a built-in QR scanner in the camera.
- Point the camera at the QR code
- Make sure the code is clear and within the frame.
- Wait for the notification
- A link or message should pop up on your screen.
- Tap the notification
- This will open the link or content in your browser or a relevant app.
- Follow the instructions on the screen
- You will be taken to a Google Maps, app where you can now click on your current location to get to your destination.

Punta Cana Nightlife

When the sun sets in Punta Cana, the destination doesn't slow down—it comes to life. As the last rays of light fade over the Caribbean Sea, a whole new side of this tropical paradise unfolds. Punta Cana's nightlife offers an exciting blend of beachside bars, lively nightclubs, intimate lounges, and cultural experiences. Whether you're a night owl seeking a place to dance the night away or looking for a romantic evening under the stars, Punta Cana has something for everyone.

In this section, we'll dive into the vibrant nightlife scene of Punta Cana, covering the best spots for drinking, dancing, and enjoying live entertainment, as well as providing tips on staying safe and navigating transportation after dark. So grab your dancing shoes (or your sandals) and get ready to explore the best places to be when the sun goes down.

Best Beach Bars, Clubs, and Lounges for Night Owls

If you love a great party atmosphere, Punta Cana is a dream come true. The area is home to a wide range of beach bars, nightclubs, and lounges that cater to all tastes. Whether you're looking for a laid-back evening with a cocktail in hand or an all-night party scene, there's something for everyone.

Mangu Disco: Dance the Night Away

For those who want to experience the heart of Punta Cana's nightlife, **Mangu Disco** is a must-visit. Located inside the **Punta Cana Hard Rock Hotel**, Mangu is known for its high-energy ambiance, featuring top-notch DJs and a mix of music genres that keep the crowd moving. From reggaeton to electronic dance music (EDM), this club has a beat for everyone, and the electric vibe makes it a popular spot for locals and tourists alike.

Mangu's dance floors are always packed, and with its lively lights and pumping beats, it's the ideal place for those who want to party until the early hours of the morning. If you're into the high-energy club scene, you won't find a better spot to dance the night away.

Coco Bongo: A Spectacle Like No Other

Coco Bongo is one of Punta Cana's most iconic nightlife venues. Famous for its extravagant shows and performances, Coco Bongo isn't just a nightclub—it's an experience. This entertainment complex blends a nightclub with a theatrical show, featuring acrobats, impersonators, dancers, and live music.

Coco Bongo's performances range from pop stars like Michael Jackson and Beyoncé to Broadway-style dance numbers. The atmosphere is electric, with confetti raining down and acrobats swinging from the rafters. It's not just a place to go dancing; it's a place to immerse yourself in a one-of-a-kind show that will leave you in awe. Whether you're with a group or enjoying a night out as a couple, Coco Bongo promises an unforgettable experience.

SCAN THE QR CODE

- Open your phone's camera app
- Most smartphones have a built-in QR scanner in the camera.
- Point the camera at the QR code
- Make sure the code is clear and within the frame.
- Wait for the notification
- A link or message should pop up on your screen.
- Tap the notification
- This will open the link or content in your browser or a relevant app.
- Follow the instructions on the screen
- You will be taken to a Google Maps, app where you can now click on your current location to get to your destination.

Onno's Bar: A Beachside Chill Vibe

If you're after a more laid-back evening with a chilled beach vibe, **Onno's Bar** is a perfect choice. Located right on the beach in **Bávaro**, Onno's offers an open-air setting where you can sip on cocktails and watch the waves roll in. This bar is famous for its relaxed atmosphere, cold drinks, and frequent live music performances, ranging from local bands to international acts.

Onno's is a favorite among tourists who want to experience Punta Cana's nightlife without the overwhelming crowds. Whether you're here for a sunset cocktail or enjoying the night with friends, Onno's offers a fun, yet more intimate experience compared to some of the larger nightclubs in the area.

Romantic Nighttime Activities: Sunset Cruises, Bonfires, and Dining

While Punta Cana's nightlife is perfect for those who want to party, it's also a great destination for couples looking to spend a romantic evening together. The warm evenings, stunning views, and variety of intimate activities make it a great spot for a romantic getaway.

Sunset Cruises: A Picture-Perfect Evening

A sunset cruise in Punta Cana is one of the most romantic experiences you can have. As the sun begins to dip below the horizon, the sky lights up with hues of pink, orange, and purple. Many tours offer private catamarans or luxury yachts that take you out onto the crystal-clear waters of the Caribbean. During the cruise, you'll enjoy spectacular views, refreshing cocktails, and the company of your loved one as the world's most beautiful sunset unfolds before your eyes.

Some tours even include a stop for a swim or a snorkeling session in the warm, turquoise waters. Whether you're looking to relax with your partner or enjoy the peacefulness of the ocean, a sunset cruise in Punta Cana is the perfect way to end the day.

Bonfires and Beachside Dining

For a truly unique experience, consider a beach bonfire dinner. Several resorts and tour companies offer private bonfires on the beach where you and your loved one can enjoy a meal under the stars, listening to the gentle waves lapping at the shore. Some dinners include romantic candle-lit settings and the chance to enjoy traditional Dominican cuisine, including fresh seafood, grilled meats, and local specialties.

The soft crackle of the fire, the cool ocean breeze, and the intimacy of a private dinner make a bonfire on the beach one of the most memorable and romantic experiences in Punta Cana.

Fine Dining at Exclusive Restaurants

Punta Cana is also home to some world-class restaurants where you can enjoy a luxurious, candle-lit dinner with your partner. From upscale seafood restaurants to authentic Dominican eateries, the culinary scene is diverse and delicious. Many of the top resorts in the area offer gourmet dining experiences with international and local cuisine, featuring fresh, locally-sourced ingredients.

If you're looking for an upscale, romantic dining experience, consider dining at **La Yola**, an upscale seafood restaurant located on a dock overlooking the water. The view of the sunset combined with the restaurant's exquisite food creates a truly unforgettable dining experience.

Local Cultural Shows and Live Entertainment

For those who want to immerse themselves in the local culture after dark, Punta Cana offers a wide range of live entertainment options. These shows allow you to experience the vibrant music, dance, and traditions that make the Dominican Republic such a unique destination.

Merengue and Bachata Shows

No visit to the Dominican Republic is complete without experiencing the nation's most iconic music genres: merengue and bachata. These energetic and rhythmic dance styles are deeply rooted in Dominican culture and are frequently performed at local venues in Punta Cana.

Many resorts and bars feature live merengue and bachata shows where dancers and musicians bring the infectious rhythm to life. If you're feeling adventurous, join in and learn a few steps yourself! There are plenty of opportunities to experience live music and even take part in a dance class, which is a great way to engage with the local culture.

Dominican Folklore Performances

For a deeper dive into Dominican culture, seek out a **Dominican folklore performance**. These shows typically feature traditional music and dance that tell the story of the Dominican Republic's history and cultural heritage. Performers wear colorful costumes and use instruments such as drums and maracas to create a lively atmosphere. These shows are perfect for anyone interested in learning more about the Dominican Republic's rich cultural traditions while enjoying a night out.

Safety Tips and Nighttime Transportation in Punta Cana

While Punta Cana offers a fantastic nightlife scene, it's important to keep safety in mind as you explore the area after dark. Here are some tips to ensure you have a fun and safe night out.

Stay in Groups and Be Aware of Your Surroundings

When out at night, always try to travel in groups, especially if you're heading to clubs or bars in unfamiliar areas. It's always a good idea to remain aware of your surroundings and stay close to friends. As with any popular tourist destination, it's best to avoid walking alone late at night, particularly in less populated areas.

Use Authorized Transportation Services

While it might be tempting to grab a ride from a local taxi or private driver, it's important to use authorized transportation services. Many resorts offer shuttle services to and from nightlife venues, and it's best to stick with these options. Alternatively, you can use reputable ride-sharing apps, such as Uber, to ensure your safety and avoid any potential issues with unlicensed drivers.

Drink Responsibly and Watch Your Belongings

As with any nightlife destination, it's important to drink responsibly and keep an eye on your belongings. Punta Cana is a safe destination overall, but it's always smart to be cautious with your valuables. Avoid leaving your phone, wallet, or other personal items unattended, and always keep them on you or locked in a secure place.

Whether you're looking to party until dawn or enjoy a romantic evening by the beach, Punta Cana's nightlife offers something for everyone. From vibrant beach bars and high-energy nightclubs to intimate dinner settings and cultural shows, there's no shortage of ways to enjoy the island's after-dark scene. Just remember to stay safe, have fun, and let Punta Cana's unforgettable nightlife experience be a highlight of your trip.

Culinary Adventures

One of the greatest pleasures of traveling to a new destination is experiencing its local cuisine, and in Punta Cana, the food is an essential part of the experience. The flavors of the Dominican Republic are rich, vibrant, and unique, combining the freshest ingredients from land and sea. Whether you're indulging in street food on the beach, savoring a multi-course meal at an upscale restaurant, or exploring local markets for authentic ingredients, there's no shortage of culinary adventures waiting for you.

Punta Cana offers a diverse food scene, from traditional Dominican dishes that are rooted in the country's history to modern twists on Caribbean flavors. In this section, we'll explore some of the must-try dishes, the best places to find them, dining options for every budget, and the local customs surrounding food. Get ready to savor the delicious tastes of the Dominican Republic, where every bite tells a story of culture, tradition, and passion.

Must-Try Dominican Dishes and Where to Find Them

The Dominican Republic is a melting pot of flavors, influenced by indigenous Taino, African, and Spanish cultures. This rich history is reflected in the country's cuisine, which is full of fresh ingredients, bold spices, and unique preparations. Here are some of the most iconic dishes you must try during your visit to Punta Cana.

Mangu: The Dominican Breakfast Classic

Start your day like a local with a plate of **mangu**, a traditional Dominican breakfast dish. Made from boiled plantains that are mashed to a creamy texture, mangu is typically served with fried eggs, salami, cheese, and avocado. It's a hearty, comforting dish that's popular with Dominicans of all ages.

You'll find mangu served at local eateries called **"comedor"** or in many resort restaurants offering Dominican breakfast options. One of the best places to enjoy mangu is **El Conuco**, a rustic restaurant in Punta Cana that specializes in authentic Dominican flavors. The atmosphere here is casual and welcoming, with live music and local artwork to set the mood.

Sancocho: A Hearty Dominican Stew

Sancocho is a rich, flavorful stew that's often considered the national dish of the Dominican Republic. It's made with a variety of meats—typically chicken, pork, and beef—and a mix of root vegetables such as yuca, potatoes, and plantains. The stew is seasoned with garlic, onions, cilantro, and other local herbs, creating a hearty and satisfying dish.

Sancocho is typically served on special occasions, but you can find it year-round at local restaurants and roadside eateries. **La Casita de Yeya** in Bávaro is a great spot to try this traditional dish, where it's served in large portions perfect for sharing with friends or family.

Mofongo: Plantain Perfection

Another plantain-based dish that's a must-try is **mofongo**. Mofongo is made by mashing fried plantains with garlic, pork cracklings, and olive oil, creating a dense, savory mound of flavor. It's often served with seafood, chicken, or beef, making it a versatile and filling dish.

You'll find mofongo at most restaurants serving Dominican cuisine, but **Mofongo House** in Punta Cana is one of the top spots for this dish. Here, they offer several variations of mofongo, including seafood mofongo, which is made with fresh, locally caught shrimp, lobster, or fish.

Pescado Frito: Fried Fish Straight from the Sea

Given Punta Cana's location along the Caribbean coast, it's no surprise that fresh seafood plays a major role in the local cuisine. **Pescado frito** (fried fish) is a popular dish made with whole fish, usually snapper or grouper, that's been seasoned and deep-fried to crispy perfection. It's typically served with a side of rice, beans, and plantains.

For some of the best pescado frito in the area, head to **Chiclayo**, a local seafood restaurant located near the water. The restaurant offers an impressive selection of fresh fish and seafood, all served with the vibrant flavors of the Dominican Republic.

La Bandera: The Dominican National Plate

No trip to Punta Cana is complete without trying **La Bandera**, which literally means "The Flag." This is the Dominican Republic's national dish and consists of rice, beans, and meat, typically accompanied by fried plantains. The dish is simple yet flavorful, and it offers a true taste of Dominican home cooking.

La Bandera can be found in almost any Dominican restaurant or comedor. It's a great option for those looking to enjoy a meal that's filling, satisfying, and deeply rooted in Dominican culture.

Dining for Every Budget: From Street Food to Fine Dining

Punta Cana is known for its luxury resorts and upscale dining experiences, but there's also an abundance of affordable options for those looking to enjoy delicious food without breaking the bank. Whether you're craving a quick bite from a street vendor or looking to indulge in a gourmet meal, Punta Cana has it all.

Street Food: Delicious, Affordable, and Authentic

If you want to truly experience the local flavors of Punta Cana, you can't miss the street food. From casual food carts to small stands near the beach, the street food scene here offers a wide range of tasty and affordable treats.

One of the most popular street foods is the **empanada**, a crispy pastry filled with various ingredients like cheese, beef, chicken, or vegetables. These hand-held snacks are perfect for a quick bite while you're out exploring. You'll also find **yuca frita** (fried yuca), **tostones** (fried green plantains), and **chicharrón** (fried pork belly) at local stands.

For an authentic street food experience, visit **Plaza Bávaro**, where you'll find a variety of vendors selling everything from empanadas to fresh coconut water.

Affordable Casual Dining: Great for Families and Groups

For those seeking a more substantial meal without the hefty price tag, there are plenty of casual dining options in Punta Cana. **La Parrillita** is a favorite among locals, offering a selection of grilled meats, fresh seafood, and traditional sides. The relaxed atmosphere and affordable prices make it a great spot for families or groups of friends.

If you're in the mood for pizza or pasta, **Capriccio Restaurant** in Bávaro offers delicious Italian dishes in a cozy, casual setting. This spot is ideal for those looking to enjoy a great meal without the fine-dining price tag.

Fine Dining: A Taste of Luxury

For those willing to indulge, Punta Cana is home to a selection of high-end restaurants that offer an unforgettable dining experience. **La Yola** at the Punta Cana Resort & Club is a standout, offering seafood dishes with a view of the ocean. The upscale setting and exceptional service make it one of the best places for a romantic dinner or a special celebration.

If you're seeking a fusion of flavors, head to **Passion by Martin Berasategui**, a Michelin-starred restaurant offering a modern twist on traditional Spanish cuisine. With its elegant atmosphere and innovative dishes, Passion is the perfect place for an unforgettable fine-dining experience.

Best Seafood Spots and Local Markets

Punta Cana's proximity to the Caribbean Sea means that fresh seafood is an integral part of the local food scene. Whether you're dining at a high-end restaurant or a casual beachside eatery, seafood is always on the menu. Here are some of the best places to enjoy fresh, delicious seafood.

Seafood Restaurants with a View

For the ultimate seafood experience, head to **Boca Marina**, a seafood restaurant located along the Punta Cana coastline. The restaurant offers a stunning view of the water and specializes in fresh fish, lobster, and other local seafood dishes. The atmosphere here is relaxed yet elegant, making it the perfect spot for a sunset dinner with a side of fresh seafood.

Visiting Local Markets for Fresh Ingredients

For those who enjoy cooking or want to bring home some local flavors, Punta Cana's local markets are a great place to find fresh seafood and other ingredients. **Plaza Lama** and **Mercado de Veron** are two of the best places to shop for fresh fish, lobster, and other seafood. You'll also find a variety of spices, herbs, and fresh produce that are essential to Dominican cooking.

Dominicans' Dining Etiquette and How to Tip

Dominican dining etiquette is relatively informal, but there are a few key points to keep in mind when dining out in Punta Cana.

- **Timing:** Lunch is typically the main meal of the day, and it's often enjoyed with family and friends around 1-2 p.m. Dinner is usually lighter and served around 7-9 p.m.

- **Tipping:** Tipping is appreciated in the Dominican Republic, and it's common to leave a 10-15% tip in restaurants. Some restaurants may include a service charge, so be sure to check your bill before tipping extra.

- **Casual Dining:** In casual dining settings, it's common for patrons to dress more relaxed, but upscale restaurants may have a smart-casual dress code, so be sure to check ahead if you're unsure.

In Punta Cana, food is more than just sustenance—it's a celebration of the country's culture, history, and passion. Whether you're indulging in street food, exploring local markets, or dining at upscale restaurants, the culinary adventures here are as diverse and unforgettable as the island itself.

Shopping in Punta Cana

A visit to Punta Cana isn't just about stunning beaches, incredible food, and adventurous activities; it's also an opportunity to bring a piece of the island home with you. Whether you're hunting for unique souvenirs to remember your trip, or you're simply curious about the local shopping scene, Punta Cana has an array of markets, malls, and boutique shops that offer everything from handcrafted jewelry to locally-made art. This section will guide you through the best places to shop, the must-have souvenirs to bring home, and how to navigate the shopping experience like a seasoned traveler.

Where to Shop: Local Markets, Malls, and Boutiques

Punta Cana boasts a variety of shopping options that cater to all tastes and budgets. From bustling local markets filled with handmade goods to luxurious malls offering international brands, there's something for everyone. Whether you prefer the authenticity of local crafts or the convenience of shopping centers, Punta Cana's shopping scene provides a wide range of experiences.

Local Markets: A Taste of Dominican Craftsmanship

For those looking to experience the heart of Dominican culture through shopping, the local markets in Punta Cana are the perfect destination. These markets are brimming with handmade goods, locally-sourced products, and unique items that can't be found in chain stores. They provide a glimpse into the artistic talent of the island's craftsmen and artisans, making them ideal for finding one-of-a-kind souvenirs.

One of the best places to visit for a true market experience is the **Bavaro Flea Market**, located in the heart of the Bavaro area. This open-air market offers a mix of local crafts, clothing, jewelry, and artwork. Vendors often sell handmade items such as intricate wood carvings, vibrant paintings, and beautiful woven baskets. A stroll through the Bavaro Flea Market is a fantastic way to soak in the local atmosphere while hunting for unique treasures.

Another notable market is the **Punta Cana Village Market**, which offers a slightly more upscale, organized shopping experience. Here, you'll find a blend of artisanal goods alongside local delicacies and souvenirs. The market features handcrafted jewelry, Dominican cigars, and local rum, which are popular items for visitors looking to bring home a piece of the island's heritage.

Malls and Boutiques: International Brands and Local Style

While the local markets offer a taste of the island's cultural heritage, Punta Cana also has a number of shopping malls and boutique stores that cater to those in search of international brands and high-end fashion. If you're looking for luxury goods, the **BlueMall Punta Cana** is one of the top shopping destinations. Located in the heart of the Bávaro area, this modern mall features a variety of upscale boutiques selling everything from designer clothing and accessories to high-end jewelry and electronics. In addition to luxury shops, BlueMall also has a selection of restaurants and cafes where you can take a break after a shopping spree.

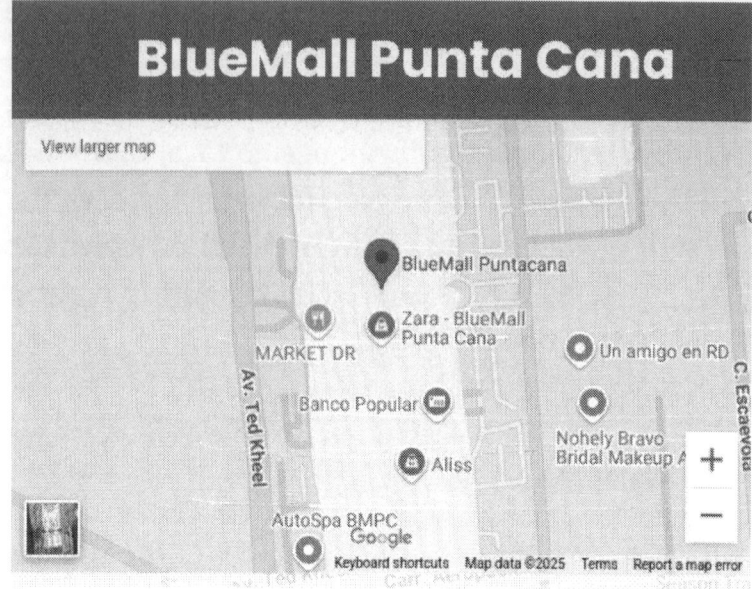

SCAN THE QR CODE

- Open your phone's camera app
- Most smartphones have a built-in QR scanner in the camera.
- Point the camera at the QR code
- Make sure the code is clear and within the frame.
- Wait for the notification
- A link or message should pop up on your screen.
- Tap the notification
- This will open the link or content in your browser or a relevant app.
- Follow the instructions on the screen
- You will be taken to a Google Maps, app where you can now click on your current location to get to your destination.

For a more casual shopping experience, **San Juan Shopping Center** is a popular choice. This mall offers a variety of stores, including clothing, electronics, and beauty products, as well as a food court and entertainment options. It's a great place to shop if you're looking for a mix of Dominican brands and international products, and it provides a comfortable, air-conditioned environment to escape the Caribbean heat.

For a truly unique shopping experience, check out the small boutiques that line the streets of Punta Cana's resorts and downtown areas. These shops often feature locally-made jewelry, artisanal clothing, and handcrafted accessories that showcase Dominican craftsmanship. Many of these stores offer personalized items, such as engraved jewelry or custom-made accessories, making them perfect for finding something special to commemorate your trip.

Unique Souvenirs to Bring Home: Rum, Cigars, Jewelry, and Art

When it comes to souvenirs, Punta Cana offers a wide variety of locally-made products that are perfect for taking home as gifts or keepsakes. Whether you're a fan of fine spirits, a cigar aficionado, or simply appreciate handcrafted art, you'll find something special to remember your time on the island.

Rum: A Taste of the Caribbean

Dominican rum is world-renowned for its smooth, rich flavor, and it's one of the most popular souvenirs that visitors bring back from Punta Cana. The Dominican Republic is home to several rum distilleries, including **Barceló**, **Brugal**, and **Atlantico**, each offering their own unique take on this Caribbean classic.

You can find rum for sale at nearly every market, boutique, and supermarket in Punta Cana. For a special touch, consider purchasing a bottle of aged rum, which is often more expensive but offers a refined flavor that's perfect for collectors or connoisseurs. If you want to take home something truly unique, seek out limited-edition or artisanal rum blends, which are often sold at distilleries or specialty shops.

Cigars: A Dominican Tradition

The Dominican Republic is one of the world's leading producers of premium cigars, and if you're a cigar lover, you won't want to miss the opportunity to bring home some of the island's finest. Cigars made in the Dominican Republic are famous for their craftsmanship and smooth taste, and you'll find them for sale at nearly every market, shop, and resort in Punta Cana.

Popular brands to look for include **Arturo Fuente**, **Davidoff**, and **Montecristo**, which are sold at cigar shops throughout the area. If you're looking for an authentic experience, visit one of the island's cigar factories for a tour and to purchase cigars directly from the source. **La Flor Dominicana** is one such factory, located near the capital, Santo Domingo, where visitors can learn about the cigar-making process and purchase cigars made on-site.

Jewelry: Handcrafted Pieces with a Story

Dominican jewelry is another popular souvenir that offers a mix of both traditional and modern styles. Local artisans craft beautiful pieces using materials like amber, larimar (a rare blue gemstone found only in the Dominican Republic), and sterling silver. Whether you're looking for a delicate necklace, an intricate bracelet, or a statement ring, there are plenty of options to choose from.

Many boutiques in Punta Cana sell jewelry made from these unique Dominican stones, and you'll find a wide variety of styles ranging from traditional designs to contemporary pieces. **La Casa del Ámbar** is a popular store that specializes in amber jewelry, offering a range of beautiful pieces that showcase the island's natural resources. For those interested in larimar jewelry, **Larimar de Dominicana** offers stunning collections that highlight the stone's distinctive blue hues.

Art: Bringing Home a Piece of the Island

For a more personal and lasting souvenir, consider purchasing a piece of Dominican art. Local artists use a variety of media, from paintings and sculptures to pottery and textiles, to create works that reflect the island's vibrant culture and natural beauty.

Galería de Arte in Punta Cana is a great place to find artwork created by local Dominican artists. You'll find colorful paintings depicting island landscapes, traditional scenes, and abstract designs, all offering a unique perspective on Dominican life. These art pieces can make a wonderful addition to your home, serving as a reminder of the beauty and culture of Punta Cana.

Price Bargaining and Shopping Etiquette

Shopping in Punta Cana is often an experience in itself, especially when visiting local markets or street vendors. While many shops in malls and boutiques have fixed prices, bargaining is common practice in local markets, and it's often expected that you'll negotiate a better deal. However, there are some unwritten rules of etiquette to keep in mind to ensure a respectful and enjoyable shopping experience.

Bargaining Tips

When shopping in local markets, start by offering a price that's lower than what the vendor initially suggests, but don't offer an insultingly low amount. A good rule of thumb is to aim for a price that's about 30-40% lower than the initial asking price, and be prepared to negotiate from there. If you're unsure of a fair price, take the time to ask around and get a sense of what similar items are being sold for at other stands.

Respectful Negotiation

Remember that bargaining is a two-way street, and the goal is to reach a price that both parties are comfortable with. Always keep the tone light and friendly, and never be aggressive or rude. If you can't agree on a price, it's perfectly fine to walk away—many vendors will call you back with a better offer if they see you're serious about making a purchase.

What to Avoid Buying as a Tourist

While Punta Cana is home to many beautiful and unique items, there are also some things that should be avoided when shopping. As a general rule, it's best to steer clear of products that are mass-produced or not representative of the local culture. Items like cheap trinkets, generic souvenirs, or low-quality knockoffs may seem like good deals at first, but they often lack authenticity and may not last long.

Additionally, be cautious when buying certain goods that may be subject to import/export restrictions, such as endangered species products or items made from restricted materials. Always check the regulations before purchasing these types of items to avoid any issues at customs.

Shopping in Punta Cana offers a unique opportunity to bring home something special from your trip, whether it's a handcrafted piece of jewelry, a bottle of world-renowned rum, or a beautiful work of art. By navigating the markets and shopping etiquette with respect, you'll find that

Punta Cana offers a vibrant and diverse shopping experience that's as rich as the island itself.

Punta Cana Day Trips & Excursions

While Punta Cana offers a world of relaxation, adventure, and entertainment within its resorts, venturing beyond the confines of your hotel can provide some of the most memorable experiences of your vacation. From pristine islands to vibrant cities, natural wonders, and thrilling adventures, the Dominican Republic is brimming with day trips and excursions that allow you to explore its rich culture, history, and stunning landscapes. Whether you're an adventure seeker, history buff, or family traveling with young children, there's something for everyone just a short distance from Punta Cana.

In this section, we'll dive into some of the best day trips and excursions, including trips to the nearby islands of Isla Saona and Isla Catalina, the bustling city of Santo Domingo, thrilling adventures in nature, and tips on booking excursions without breaking the bank.

Exploring Isla Saona, Isla Catalina, and Santo Domingo

Isla Saona: A Tropical Paradise

No trip to Punta Cana would be complete without a visit to **Isla Saona**, one of the Dominican Republic's most stunning and iconic destinations. Situated just off the southeastern coast, this idyllic island is part of the **East National Park** and is renowned for its crystal-clear waters, white sandy beaches, and lush palm trees. The island is a popular day trip destination and can be reached by boat, with several tours available from Punta Cana.

The day trip to Isla Saona typically includes a scenic boat ride through the turquoise waters of the Caribbean, often with a stop at **Canto de la**

Playa, a sandbar in the middle of the sea, where visitors can enjoy swimming, snorkeling, and sunbathing in a truly unique setting. The island itself offers a serene escape from the hustle and bustle of the resort areas. Here, visitors can enjoy the island's pristine beaches, indulge in a delicious local seafood lunch, and explore the surrounding natural beauty.

Isla Saona is a haven for nature lovers, with abundant wildlife, including tropical birds and marine life. For those who enjoy snorkeling, the waters surrounding the island are teeming with vibrant coral reefs and colorful fish. Many tours also offer opportunities to visit the **natural pool**, a shallow area where starfish can be seen in their natural habitat.

Isla Catalina: A Hidden Gem for Snorkeling and Relaxation

Another must-see island near Punta Cana is **Isla Catalina**, known for its peaceful and uncrowded beaches, clear waters, and fantastic snorkeling opportunities. Located just a short boat ride from the mainland, Isla Catalina is a small island that offers a more secluded, laid-back experience compared to Isla Saona. Its quiet charm makes it the perfect destination for those seeking a tranquil escape, far from the larger crowds.

The island is famous for its underwater attractions, particularly **Catalina Wall**, a popular diving and snorkeling spot. The waters around Isla Catalina are home to coral reefs, colorful fish, and even the occasional sea turtle, making it an ideal destination for marine enthusiasts. Many tours to Isla Catalina include snorkeling trips, allowing visitors to explore the vibrant underwater world in a safe and controlled environment.

In addition to snorkeling, Isla Catalina offers beautiful beaches for lounging, relaxing, and taking in the spectacular natural surroundings. With fewer visitors than other islands, it's an excellent place to escape the crowds and enjoy a quiet day in paradise.

Santo Domingo: Immerse Yourself in the History and Culture

For those looking to dive deeper into the history and culture of the Dominican Republic, a day trip to **Santo Domingo**, the capital city, is a must. Located about 2.5 hours from Punta Cana, Santo Domingo is the oldest continuously inhabited

European settlement in the Americas, offering visitors a chance to explore centuries of history in its colonial architecture, museums, and vibrant streets.

The heart of Santo Domingo's historical district is **Zona Colonial**, a UNESCO World Heritage site filled with cobblestone streets, colonial buildings, and historical landmarks. Notable sites include the **Alcázar de Colón**, the former residence of Christopher Columbus's son, Diego, and the **Cathedral of Santa María la Menor**, the oldest cathedral in the Americas. Walking through this area feels like stepping back in time, and it provides a fascinating glimpse into the country's colonial past.

In addition to the historical sites, Santo Domingo is also home to bustling markets, vibrant local neighborhoods, and delicious restaurants offering authentic Dominican cuisine. Whether you're wandering through the colorful streets or enjoying a traditional Dominican meal, a visit to Santo Domingo provides a perfect blend of culture, history, and modern life.

Adventure Trips: Caves, Waterfalls, and Hidden Natural Wonders

Cave Tours: Explore the Mysteries of the Dominican Landscape

For nature lovers and adventure seekers, the Dominican Republic is home to some of the most impressive natural caves in the Caribbean. One of the best ways to experience the country's natural beauty is by taking a guided cave tour.

The Cueva de las Maravillas (Cave of Wonders) is one of the most famous caves in the Dominican Republic. Located about an hour's drive from Punta Cana, this cave is known for its ancient petroglyphs and pictographs created by the Taino, the indigenous people of the island. The cave is a marvel of both history and nature, with impressive stalactites and stalagmites decorating the interior. Guided tours provide insight into the cave's history and its significance to the Taino people, making it a unique and educational experience.

Another exciting cave adventure is a trip to the **Cueva de Padre Nuestro** (Father Our Cave), which is located within the **National Park of the East**. This cave is part of a larger system that includes underground rivers and an array of stalactite and stalagmite formations. The tour typically includes a hike through the park, giving you the chance to witness the beauty of the Dominican jungle before entering the cave.

Waterfalls and Natural Springs: A Refreshing Adventure

For those who love the outdoors, the Dominican Republic offers plenty of opportunities to explore waterfalls and hidden natural springs. One of the most popular spots for a waterfall excursion is **El Limón Waterfall**, located in the Samana Peninsula.

This stunning 165-foot waterfall is surrounded by lush greenery and can be reached by horseback or on foot. The hike to the waterfall is a thrilling adventure in itself, and once you reach the falls, you can take a refreshing dip in the natural pool below.

Another great waterfall to visit is **Damajagua Falls**, also known as the **27 Waterfalls**. Located in the northern part of the country, these falls consist of 27 separate waterfalls cascading down a series of limestone steps. Visitors can hike, swim, and jump into the natural pools, making it an ideal adventure for adrenaline junkies and nature lovers alike.

Family-Friendly Excursions and Group Tours

While many of Punta Cana's day trips cater to adventurous travelers, there are also plenty of family-friendly excursions that are perfect for those traveling with children or large groups. Whether you're looking to explore the local wildlife, enjoy a fun day at an amusement park, or simply relax on a private beach, Punta Cana offers plenty of options for families and groups of all ages.

Family Adventures at the Dolphin Encounter

One of the top family-friendly activities in Punta Cana is the **Dolphin Encounter** at **Dolphin Explorer**. This interactive experience allows families to swim and play with dolphins in a safe and controlled environment. The program is designed for all ages, so even young children can participate in the fun. It's a memorable experience for animal lovers and provides an opportunity to learn about the importance of marine conservation.

Group Tours: Discover Punta Cana Together

If you're traveling with a group, consider booking a guided tour that allows everyone to experience the best of Punta Cana together. Many tour operators offer group excursions that include visits to nearby islands, cultural landmarks, and natural attractions. These tours often include a knowledgeable guide, transportation, and lunch, making it an easy and convenient way to explore the region without the hassle of planning logistics.

Tips for Booking the Best Day Trips Without Overpaying

Booking day trips and excursions in Punta Cana is simple, but it's important to know how to get the best value for your money. To ensure you don't overpay, consider these helpful tips:

Book in Advance

Many popular excursions can fill up quickly, especially during the peak travel seasons. To secure the best prices and ensure availability, it's a good idea to book your excursions ahead of time. Many tour operators offer discounts for early bookings, so check online for deals before you arrive in Punta Cana.

Compare Prices

Different tour operators may offer similar excursions at varying price points. Take the time to compare prices and read reviews to ensure you're getting a fair deal. Keep in mind that while some tours may seem more expensive, they may include extra perks like meals, drinks, and additional activities that make the experience worth the price.

Check for Hidden Fees

When booking tours, always ask about additional fees or charges that may not be included in the initial price. Some excursions may have extra costs for equipment rental, entrance fees, or transportation. Make sure to ask about all costs upfront to avoid surprises later.

Punta Cana's day trips and excursions are an excellent way to experience the diverse beauty and culture of the Dominican Republic. Whether you're exploring secluded islands, hiking to hidden waterfalls, or immersing yourself in the island's rich history, there's something for everyone. By choosing the right tours and booking wisely, you can make the most of your time in Punta Cana and create unforgettable memories.

Traveling Around Punta Cana

Navigating a new destination can often be one of the trickiest parts of a trip. Whether you're soaking in the sun on the beach or exploring the local culture, getting around Punta Cana should be as easy and stress-free as possible. Fortunately, Punta Cana offers various transportation options that suit different needs, from taxis and Ubers to car rentals and alternative modes of transport. Each option comes with its own set of advantages and considerations, and understanding the best way to travel around the area will help you maximize your time on the island.

In this section, we will cover everything you need to know about transportation in Punta Cana, including the pros and cons of taxis, Ubers, and public transportation, tips for renting cars, how to reach hidden spots with local hacks, and alternative transport options like walking and cycling.

Navigating Punta Cana: Taxis, Uber, and Public Transport

Taxis in Punta Cana: A Convenient, Yet Costly Option

Taxis are one of the most common modes of transportation in Punta Cana, especially for those who prefer a direct and private ride. They are readily available throughout the city, including at the airport, resorts, and popular tourist spots. While they offer a convenient way to get from one location to another, taxis in Punta Cana come with a few caveats that you should be aware of.

One of the main issues with taxis is the price. Unlike many cities where fares are metered, taxi prices in Punta Cana are often negotiated upfront or set by zone, meaning you need to agree on the fare before starting the ride. This can sometimes lead to overpaying, especially for tourists who are unfamiliar with the typical rates. To avoid this, it's important to confirm the price before getting in the cab. You may also want to ask your hotel concierge for approximate rates to help guide your negotiations.

Another thing to keep in mind is that taxi drivers may not always speak fluent English, so having a basic understanding of Spanish or using a translation app can help bridge the language gap. However, taxis remain one of the easiest and fastest ways to travel in Punta Cana, especially if you need to go to a specific destination directly from the airport or a resort.

Uber: A Convenient and Cost-Effective Option

For those who prefer a more predictable and often cheaper transportation option, **Uber** is available in Punta Cana, and it has gained popularity among both tourists and locals. The benefits of using Uber in Punta Cana include transparent pricing, ease of use via the app, and the ability to track your ride. This can be especially comforting for travelers who are concerned about overpaying for taxi rides or navigating an unfamiliar city.

Using Uber is simple—download the app, enter your destination, and wait for a nearby driver to accept your ride. One of the biggest advantages of Uber over traditional taxis is the ability to see an estimated fare before you even request a ride. Additionally, Uber drivers in Punta Cana tend to be well-rated and provide a higher level of comfort and professionalism than some local taxi services.

However, there are a few considerations when using Uber in Punta Cana. While Uber is widely used in the major tourist areas like Punta Cana Village, Bávaro, and the hotel zone, there are some locations where Uber availability may be more limited. It's also important to note that Uber rides in Punta Cana can sometimes be more expensive during peak times or when demand is high, so it's wise to plan accordingly.

Public Transportation: A More Local Option, But Not for Everyone

Public transportation in Punta Cana is available but not as widely used by tourists. The most common form of public transport is the **guagua**, a small, shared minibus that travels along set routes throughout the region. These buses are an inexpensive way to get around, but they can be crowded and may not always be the most comfortable or reliable option for tourists who are unfamiliar with the local routes.

Guaguas can be a good option for those looking to immerse themselves in the local culture or for budget-conscious travelers who don't mind navigating the local transportation system. However, if you're on a tight schedule or seeking comfort, public transportation might not be your best bet. In addition, these buses often make multiple stops along the way, which can significantly extend travel time.

If you do choose to take public transportation, be sure to have some cash on hand, as guaguas typically don't accept credit cards. Keep in mind that the buses may not always run on a strict timetable, so it's important to factor in some extra time for your journey.

Renting Cars: Pros, Cons, and Safety Considerations

The Pros of Renting a Car in Punta Cana

Renting a car in Punta Cana can offer a high level of freedom and flexibility, especially if you plan to explore areas outside of the typical tourist destinations. It allows you to visit more remote parts of the island at your own pace, such as the **Samana Peninsula**, **Higuey**, or hidden beaches, all without relying on organized tours or public transport.

If you're planning on taking day trips or visiting multiple spots throughout the island, having a rental car can be extremely convenient. Most car rental agencies offer a variety of vehicles to choose from, from compact cars to larger SUVs and 4x4s, which can be useful for navigating the more rugged roads in some parts of the country.

Another advantage of renting a car is the potential for cost savings. If you're traveling with a group or planning to stay in Punta Cana for an extended period, renting a car may prove more economical than constantly relying on taxis or ridesharing services, especially if you plan on traveling long distances.

The Cons of Renting a Car in Punta Cana

While renting a car in Punta Cana provides plenty of freedom, there are also some downsides to consider. One of the biggest challenges is driving in unfamiliar conditions. Roads in the Dominican Republic may not always be well-maintained, and traffic can be chaotic, particularly in busy areas or during peak hours. Many tourists may find themselves unprepared for the local driving habits, which can seem a bit aggressive compared to what they're used to back home.

Additionally, rental cars can be expensive, especially when you factor in insurance, fuel, and additional fees. Some rental agencies may also require a deposit, which could tie up funds during your trip. And while driving is generally safe, it's important to be aware of local traffic laws and always exercise caution on the roads.

Lastly, parking can be a challenge in certain areas, particularly around popular tourist spots or busy beach towns. Finding a secure and safe parking spot may require some effort, especially in more crowded areas.

Safety Considerations

If you choose to rent a car in Punta Cana, it's important to stay vigilant. Be sure to check your rental vehicle for any existing damages before leaving the lot to avoid being held responsible for them later. Additionally, it's highly recommended to opt for comprehensive insurance coverage, as this can provide peace of mind in case of any incidents.

Always lock your car when leaving it unattended and avoid leaving valuables inside, as petty theft can occur in some areas. Be especially cautious when driving at night or in unfamiliar regions, as the roads may not be well-lit and local driving practices may be unpredictable.

Getting to the Best Hidden Spots: Local Transportation Hacks

One of the biggest advantages of staying in Punta Cana is the proximity to hidden gems and less-visited attractions that many tourists overlook. Getting to these spots, however, often requires a bit of local know-how. Here are a few tips to help you explore beyond the main tourist hotspots:

Public Motoconchos: Motorcycle Taxis

If you're looking to venture off the beaten path, consider using **motoconchos**, or motorcycle taxis, which are commonly used by locals to navigate the smaller, less accessible roads. These quick and affordable rides can take you to places that may not be easily reached by car or taxi. However, motoconchos aren't always the safest option for inexperienced riders, so use them cautiously and only with reputable drivers.

Shared Taxis and Group Rides

If you're traveling in a group and want to save money, consider using **shared taxis** or organizing group rides to more remote locations. Many taxi drivers offer group rates for multiple passengers, so you can often negotiate a better price if you're traveling with others. Local hotels and resorts may also help arrange these rides for you.

Walking, Cycling, and Other Alternative Transport Options

For those looking to explore the area in a more eco-friendly or adventurous way, walking and cycling are great alternatives. Punta Cana's weather is typically warm and sunny, making it perfect for outdoor activities. Many hotels provide bicycles for guests, and there are several biking paths in more developed areas.

Walking is also a viable option for short trips to local attractions or beaches. Just be sure to stay hydrated and wear sunscreen, as the sun can be intense throughout the day.

In summary, there are plenty of transportation options in Punta Cana, each with its own pros and cons. Whether you're opting for a taxi, using Uber, renting a car, or trying something more adventurous like motoconchos, the key to enjoying your trip is to understand your options and plan ahead. With the right transportation strategy, you can explore the best that Punta Cana has to offer while ensuring a smooth, safe, and enjoyable experience.

Punta Cana for Families, and Solo Travelers

Punta Cana is a destination that caters to a wide range of travelers, whether you're visiting with your family, embarking on a romantic getaway, traveling solo, or planning a group trip with friends. Each type of traveler will find something special to make their experience memorable. With its pristine beaches, rich culture, and diverse activities, Punta Cana offers something for everyone. In this section, we will explore the best options for families, couples, solo travelers, and group trips, ensuring that no matter your travel style, you'll know exactly where to go and what to do.

Best Family Resorts, Kids' Clubs, and Child-Friendly Activities

Punta Cana is a fantastic destination for families, offering a wide range of resorts and activities designed to keep both adults and children entertained. When choosing a family-friendly resort, it's important to look for amenities that cater to children's needs, such as kids' clubs, child-friendly pools, and organized activities that allow the adults to have some relaxation time as well.

Family-Friendly Resorts in Punta Cana

Many resorts in Punta Cana specialize in family vacations, providing all-inclusive packages that include meals, drinks, activities, and childcare. Resorts like the **Nickelodeon Hotels & Resorts Punta Cana** offer a fun, interactive environment for kids with character meet-and-greets, water parks, and activities that revolve around popular shows and characters. For families seeking more relaxation, resorts like **The Reserve at Paradisus Palma Real** or **Hard Rock Hotel & Casino Punta Cana** provide plenty of amenities, including spacious family suites, kids' pools, and family-focused excursions.

Kids' Clubs and Child-Centered Activities

One of the highlights of a family vacation in Punta Cana is the variety of kids' clubs and activities available at the resorts. These clubs are designed to keep children engaged with arts and crafts, water sports, beach games, and even educational activities that highlight the local culture. Many resorts offer specialized clubs based on age groups, ranging from toddlers to teenagers, ensuring that every child has age-appropriate activities to enjoy.

For example, the **Bahia Principe Luxury Ambar** offers a kids' club for children aged 4-12, which includes themed days and interactive experiences. For younger children, resorts like **Club Med Punta Cana** provide childcare services that include supervised playtime and nap sessions, allowing parents to enjoy some much-needed downtime.

Child-Friendly Activities Outside the Resort

While the resort amenities are fantastic, Punta Cana offers a wealth of activities beyond the hotel grounds that are perfect for families. For those who love animals, the **Dolphin Explorer** experience allows families to swim with dolphins, sea lions, and other marine life. There are also excursions to the **Indigenous Eyes Ecological Park**, where families can explore nature trails, visit freshwater lagoons, and learn about local wildlife in a safe and educational environment.

Families with older children or teenagers may also enjoy an adventure-filled day at the **Scape Park**, a natural theme park that offers ziplining, cave exploration, and a chance to swim in cenotes.

Whether your children love nature, animals, or adventure, Punta Cana offers an array of options to create lasting memories.

Romantic Getaways: Secluded Resorts, Private Dinners, and Honeymoon Ideas

Punta Cana is an idyllic destination for couples seeking romance and intimacy. Whether you're planning a honeymoon, celebrating an anniversary, or simply looking for a romantic escape, Punta Cana offers a variety of secluded resorts, private activities, and intimate experiences that cater to couples looking to relax and enjoy each other's company in a beautiful setting.

Secluded Resorts and Private Villas

For couples who want to enjoy privacy and luxury, Punta Cana has some of the most stunning resorts that provide the perfect blend of romance and relaxation. Resorts like the **Eden Roc Cap Cana** and **Zoetry Agua Punta Cana** offer private villas, beachfront suites, and personalized services tailored for couples. These resorts are known for their intimate atmospheres, private beaches, and world-class amenities, ensuring that couples have a peaceful and luxurious escape.

Many of these resorts also offer romantic packages that include private dinners on the beach, couples' spa treatments, and excursions designed for two, such as sunset boat rides or secluded picnics in beautiful locations.

Private Dinners and Sunset Cruises

No romantic getaway is complete without a special dining experience. Punta Cana offers several options for private, romantic dinners. Many resorts offer beachfront dining experiences where couples can enjoy a candlelit meal with the sound of the waves as a backdrop. For an even more intimate experience, consider booking a private dinner aboard a luxury yacht or a catamaran, where you can sail along the coast while enjoying a gourmet meal as the sun sets over the Caribbean.

Another must-do romantic activity is taking a sunset cruise. Many operators offer romantic boat tours that include drinks, snacks, and a relaxing ambiance. Watching the sun dip below the horizon while surrounded by the sparkling blue waters is an experience that will make any couple feel like they're in paradise.

Honeymoon Ideas and Exclusive Experiences

For newlyweds, Punta Cana offers a variety of honeymoon packages designed to make your first trip as a married couple unforgettable. Many resorts offer honeymoon suites with private pools, champagne upon arrival, and spa treatments designed for two. These packages often include romantic extras such as couples' massages, private excursions, and other exclusive perks.

Couples who are looking for adventure can also enjoy some of the many outdoor experiences Punta Cana has to offer, such as horseback riding along the beach, ziplining through lush forests, or a day trip to the picturesque **Saona Island**.

Solo Travel in Punta Cana: What to Do, Where to Go, and How to Stay Safe

Punta Cana is not just for families and couples; it's also an ideal destination for solo travelers. Whether you're seeking a quiet retreat, an adventure-filled holiday, or a chance to meet new people, Punta Cana offers a wide range of activities and experiences that are perfect for those traveling alone.

What to Do as a Solo Traveler

For solo travelers, Punta Cana offers a variety of experiences, whether you're seeking relaxation or adventure. If you're looking to unwind and recharge, spend some time at one of the area's world-class spas, indulge in yoga on the beach, or enjoy a day lounging by the pool or on the sand. Many resorts offer yoga and wellness classes specifically designed for solo travelers looking to focus on their health and well-being.

For those seeking more active pursuits, Punta Cana offers activities like water sports, hiking, and exploring the natural beauty of the region. Solo travelers often enjoy excursions to **Hoyo Azul**, a beautiful freshwater lagoon tucked into the Dominican jungle, where you can swim and explore in peace.

If you enjoy meeting new people, many resorts host group activities such as cooking classes, dance lessons, and themed parties, where solo travelers can connect with others. Additionally, Punta Cana has a vibrant social scene, with plenty of bars, cafes, and nightclubs where solo travelers can mingle.

Safety Tips for Solo Travelers

While Punta Cana is generally a safe destination, it's always important to stay vigilant when traveling solo. Stick to well-lit areas at night, avoid walking alone in isolated parts of the city, and be cautious when engaging with street vendors or unfamiliar people. If you're staying in a resort, always use the safe in your room for valuables, and keep your passport and other important documents in a secure place.

It's also a good idea to book excursions through your resort or reputable tour operators to ensure that you're in safe hands. If you plan to rent a car or use public transportation, always take extra care to familiarize yourself with your route and ask locals for recommendations if needed.

Group Travel: Tips for Smooth Group Getaways

Punta Cana is a fantastic destination for group travel, whether you're organizing a family reunion, a destination wedding, or a getaway with friends. The area offers plenty of activities that appeal to large groups, making it easy to plan a trip that everyone will enjoy.

Group-Friendly Resorts

When traveling with a large group, choosing the right resort is key. Many all-inclusive resorts in Punta Cana cater specifically to group travel. These resorts offer spacious accommodations, group activities, and team-building experiences, ensuring that your entire group has a memorable time. Resorts like the **Dreams Palm Beach Punta Cana** and **Barceló Bávaro Palace** are popular for their wide array of group-friendly amenities, including group dining options, private event spaces, and group tours.

Planning Group Activities

Punta Cana offers a range of group activities, from private boat tours to ziplining adventures. Consider booking a private catamaran cruise for your group, where you can enjoy the beautiful coastline and Caribbean waters together. Alternatively, group excursions to places like **Saona Island** or **Scape Park** allow everyone to bond over exciting adventures like hiking, snorkeling, or exploring hidden caves.

One of the best things about Punta Cana is that it offers something for everyone in your group, regardless of age or interest. Whether you want a quiet day at the spa or an adrenaline-pumping adventure, you'll find plenty of options that cater to all tastes and preferences.

Group Travel Tips

When organizing a group trip, it's important to communicate and plan in advance. Establish a list of everyone's preferences for activities, accommodations, and dining, and try to accommodate as many people as possible. It's also a good idea to set up a group chat or communication platform so that everyone can stay informed during the trip.

Punta Cana's excellent infrastructure and wide range of services make it an ideal destination for any type of group, whether you're looking for adventure, relaxation, or bonding time.

Sustainable Travel in Punta Cana

In recent years, sustainable travel has become an essential focus for many destinations around the world, and Punta Cana is no exception. As tourism continues to thrive in this tropical paradise, there has been a growing movement to ensure that tourism benefits both the environment and the local communities. By choosing eco-friendly resorts, supporting responsible businesses, and engaging in wildlife conservation efforts, travelers can enjoy their vacation while minimizing their impact on this stunning destination. In this section, we'll explore the various ways that visitors to Punta Cana can travel responsibly, from staying at eco-conscious resorts to supporting local conservation initiatives.

Eco-Conscious Resorts, Restaurants, and Activities

Punta Cana boasts a range of eco-friendly resorts and businesses that prioritize sustainability while offering guests the luxury and comfort they expect. Many of these establishments have adopted practices aimed at reducing waste, conserving water, and preserving the natural beauty of the region, while also ensuring that local communities benefit from tourism. Here, we'll highlight some of the key eco-conscious choices for travelers who want to support sustainable tourism during their stay in Punta Cana.

Eco-Friendly Resorts

For travelers seeking to minimize their environmental footprint, Punta Cana offers several eco-conscious resorts that integrate sustainable practices into their operations. Resorts such as the **Eden Roc Cap Cana** and **AlSol Tiara Cap Cana** are committed to reducing their carbon footprint by using renewable energy, limiting plastic use, and conserving water. These resorts focus on sustainable design, using locally sourced materials, and integrating native plant life into their landscaping, which not only enhances the aesthetic but also supports biodiversity.

Another example is the **Zoetry Agua Punta Cana**, which prides itself on being an eco-resort that minimizes waste, promotes sustainable farming practices, and provides guests with organic and locally sourced food. Many of these resorts are also committed to sustainable architecture, utilizing energy-efficient systems for cooling and lighting, and ensuring that their operations have minimal environmental impact.

These resorts not only offer guests luxurious accommodations but also provide the opportunity to experience the beauty of Punta Cana in an eco-conscious way. Guests can enjoy private beaches, rejuvenating spa treatments, and fine dining, all while knowing that their stay supports environmental sustainability.

Sustainable Restaurants

Dining is an integral part of the Punta Cana experience, and there are several restaurants and eateries that focus on sustainable sourcing and eco-friendly practices. Restaurants like **La Yola** and **The Beach Club** at **Eden Roc** serve locally sourced seafood, vegetables, and fruits, supporting both local farmers and the fishing community. These restaurants also avoid plastic packaging and strive to minimize waste by composting and recycling.

In addition to sourcing ingredients sustainably, many of these restaurants also use eco-friendly materials for their furnishings and utensils, ensuring that even the dining experience adheres to sustainability principles. By choosing these types of eateries, travelers not only enjoy delicious food but also contribute to the health and well-being of the local environment and economy.

Eco-Friendly Activities

Beyond resorts and dining, Punta Cana offers a wealth of activities that allow visitors to enjoy the natural beauty of the region while minimizing their environmental impact. Several tour companies in the area offer eco-tours that highlight the region's biodiversity and natural ecosystems. Visitors can explore the **Indigenous Eyes Ecological Park**, which is dedicated to the conservation of native plants and animals, or embark on a guided tour of the **Hoyo Azul** natural lagoon, where they can swim in crystal-clear waters surrounded by lush vegetation. These eco-tours promote environmental awareness and give travelers a deeper understanding of the importance of preserving Punta Cana's natural resources.

Water Sports and Sustainable Adventures

For those who enjoy adventure sports, there are eco-friendly water activities like snorkeling, paddleboarding, and kayaking, where equipment is often made from sustainable materials. Many operators also emphasize responsible practices, such as avoiding damage to coral reefs and marine life, ensuring that these activities do not negatively impact the local ecosystem.

How to Support Local Communities and Sustainable Businesses

One of the most important aspects of responsible tourism is supporting local communities and ensuring that tourism dollars benefit the people who call Punta Cana home. By choosing locally-owned businesses, supporting artisan shops, and engaging in community-based tourism experiences, visitors can make a positive impact on the region and help preserve the cultural integrity of the area.

Supporting Local Artisans

Punta Cana is home to a vibrant artisan community that creates beautiful crafts, jewelry, and textiles. Visitors can support these artisans by purchasing handmade goods from local markets, shops, and vendors. Items like handwoven baskets, hand-carved wooden figurines, and vibrant paintings all help sustain local businesses and provide a livelihood for artisans.

Additionally, many of these artisans use sustainable materials, ensuring that their products have a minimal environmental impact. By purchasing locally-made goods, travelers can contribute directly to the community's economic growth while also supporting sustainable practices.

Community-Based Tourism Initiatives

Punta Cana is increasingly seeing the rise of community-based tourism, which offers visitors the opportunity to engage directly with local communities and experience their culture in a meaningful way. Programs such as cultural workshops, cooking classes, and village tours allow tourists to gain insight into the daily lives of the Dominican people while supporting local economies.

For example, the **Cultural Tour of Higuey** gives visitors the chance to explore the nearby town, visit local markets, and engage in traditional Dominican activities, all while ensuring that the proceeds go directly to the community. These types of experiences not only help preserve local customs but also empower local residents to benefit from tourism in a sustainable and equitable manner.

Eco-Friendly Shopping

When shopping for souvenirs in Punta Cana, it's important to consider the environmental and social impact of your purchases. Opting for handmade items crafted by local artisans, instead of mass-produced souvenirs, helps ensure that the community benefits directly from the sale. Look for stores and vendors that prioritize sustainable sourcing and avoid purchasing items made from endangered species, such as coral, tortoiseshell, or certain types of wood.

Wildlife Conservation and Responsible Animal Encounters

Punta Cana is home to a wide variety of wildlife, including marine life, birds, and land animals. Protecting these creatures and their habitats is crucial to maintaining the region's natural beauty and biodiversity. Responsible animal encounters, where tourists can interact with wildlife in a way that supports their well-being, are an important part of sustainable tourism in Punta Cana.

Responsible Wildlife Tours

Several eco-conscious operators in Punta Cana offer wildlife tours that prioritize animal welfare and conservation. For example, when participating in a dolphin encounter, it's important to choose a tour operator that ensures the dolphins are treated ethically and live in natural habitats. Dolphin Explorer, for instance, is committed to providing a responsible environment for its dolphins, offering educational experiences rather than exploitative interactions.

Additionally, there are many opportunities to engage in marine conservation efforts, such as guided snorkeling trips where tourists learn about coral reef preservation and the importance of protecting marine species. These tours help raise awareness of environmental issues and contribute to ongoing conservation work in the region.

Avoiding Animal Exploitation

As with many popular tourist destinations, Punta Cana also faces the challenge of animal exploitation for entertainment purposes. As a responsible traveler, it's important to avoid participating in activities that harm animals or force them to perform unnatural behaviors, such as elephant rides or staged animal performances. Instead, choose activities that promote conservation and educate visitors about the importance of protecting wildlife.

By being discerning about the animal experiences you choose, you can ensure that your interactions are ethical and contribute positively to the local wildlife population.

Reducing Your Carbon Footprint While Visiting Punta Cana

While enjoying all that Punta Cana has to offer, it's important to be mindful of your carbon footprint. There are several ways that travelers can minimize their environmental impact during their stay, from reducing energy consumption to choosing sustainable transportation options.

Sustainable Transportation

One of the easiest ways to reduce your carbon footprint in Punta Cana is by opting for sustainable modes of transportation. Instead of renting a car or using private taxis for every journey, consider using public transportation or shared rides like **Uber** or **Lyft**. These options help reduce the number of vehicles on the road and can be a more eco-friendly alternative to driving alone.

Additionally, many resorts offer bike rentals, which allow you to explore the area in a low-impact way while enjoying the beautiful scenery. For short trips, consider walking to nearby attractions, which not only reduces your carbon footprint but also gives you a chance to immerse yourself in the local culture.

Energy Conservation

While staying at an eco-conscious resort, be mindful of your energy consumption by turning off lights, air conditioning, and electronics when not in use. Many resorts also provide guests with the option to reduce their environmental impact by reusing towels and linens, so take advantage of these sustainable practices to help conserve water and energy.

Eco-Tourism Certifications

When booking your activities or accommodations, look for eco-tourism certifications or labels, such as the **Green Globe** certification or **Rainforest Alliance** certification. These certifications indicate that a business is committed to sustainable practices and environmental responsibility. By supporting these certified establishments, you're ensuring that your travel choices align with your values of sustainability and conservation.

Conclusion

Punta Cana, with its stunning beaches, lush landscapes, and rich culture, remains one of the most sought-after destinations in the Caribbean. Whether you're planning a relaxing beach vacation, an adventurous exploration of natural wonders, or a deep dive into local culture, Punta Cana offers an abundance of experiences for every type of traveler. As you prepare for your 2025 adventure, it's important to keep in mind the essential tips and advice that will help you maximize your time in this tropical paradise. In this final section, we'll recap the key points of your Punta Cana journey, offer practical packing advice, and provide you with a checklist to ensure you're fully prepared for your trip.

Recap of Essential Travel Tips for Your Punta Cana Journey

To make the most of your Punta Cana experience, a bit of preparation goes a long way. Throughout this guide, we've covered a variety of essential tips for navigating Punta Cana, from sustainable travel practices to recommendations for dining, shopping, and exploring beyond the resorts. Here's a quick recap of the most important travel advice to keep in mind:

- **Plan Ahead for Popular Activities**: Punta Cana is a popular destination, and some activities, such as boat tours, excursions, and spa appointments, can fill up quickly. It's wise to book these in advance, especially if you have specific experiences in mind that you don't want to miss.

- **Respect Local Customs**: Dominican Republic culture is warm and welcoming, but it's also important to be mindful of local customs. Dress modestly when visiting churches or rural areas, and always ask before taking photos of locals, especially in rural communities or at traditional events.

- **Stay Hydrated and Protect Yourself from the Sun**: The tropical climate in Punta Cana can be intense, so it's crucial to drink plenty of water throughout the day. Don't forget to apply sunscreen regularly, especially if you plan to spend time outdoors. Wearing a hat and sunglasses can also help shield you from the sun's rays.

- **Opt for Sustainable Travel**: From eco-friendly resorts to community-based tourism, Punta Cana is increasingly offering options for sustainable travel. Consider staying at resorts and supporting businesses that prioritize environmental responsibility and local community development.

- **Be Aware of the Weather**: While Punta Cana is generally sunny and warm, it's important to be aware of the seasonal weather patterns. The rainy season typically runs from May to October, so if you're visiting during this time, be prepared for occasional afternoon showers.

By keeping these tips in mind, you'll be well-equipped to navigate Punta Cana's vibrant culture and stunning landscapes with ease and confidence.

Packing for Punta Cana: Essentials for Every Type of Traveler

Packing for Punta Cana can be relatively simple, but it's essential to ensure you have everything you need to make the most of your vacation. The destination's tropical climate calls for lightweight clothing, sun protection, and the right gear for your chosen activities. Here's a guide to the essentials to pack for your Punta Cana trip, tailored for different types of travelers:

For the Beach Lover

- **Swimwear**: Pack several swimsuits for lounging on the beach, swimming in pools, or enjoying water sports. Quick-dry fabrics are ideal for easy transitions between the beach and your hotel room.

- **Sunscreen**: Choose a broad-spectrum sunscreen with high SPF to protect your skin from the intense Caribbean sun. Don't forget to bring lip balm with SPF protection as well.

- **Flip-Flops and Beach Shoes**: Comfortable sandals or flip-flops are essential for walking along the beach and around your resort.

- **Beach Bag**: A lightweight, water-resistant bag to carry your beach essentials, such as towels, sunscreen, sunglasses, and books.

- **Hat and Sunglasses**: A wide-brimmed hat or cap and a pair of sunglasses will help shield your face and eyes from the sun.

For the Adventurer

- **Activewear**: If you plan to explore Punta Cana's natural wonders, pack comfortable activewear for hiking, biking, or other outdoor activities. Lightweight and moisture-wicking fabrics will keep you cool during strenuous excursions.

- **Water Shoes**: If you're venturing into caves, waterfalls, or the ocean, water shoes are a must-have to protect your feet while keeping them comfortable.

- **Camera**: Capture memories of your adventure, whether you're snorkeling in crystal-clear waters or hiking to a scenic viewpoint. A waterproof camera or phone case is a great investment if you plan on being near water.

For the Culture Seeker

- **Modest Clothing**: When visiting local towns, religious sites, or rural areas, it's advisable to dress conservatively. A couple of long skirts or pants and tops with sleeves can help you respect local customs.

- **Comfortable Walking Shoes**: Whether you're exploring the streets of Santo Domingo or walking around local markets, comfortable shoes are essential for cultural sightseeing.

- **Notebook or Journal**: If you love to document your travels, a small notebook or journal can be a great way to capture your thoughts and reflections as you immerse yourself in Punta Cana's culture.

For the Family

- **Child-Friendly Essentials**: If you're traveling with young children, don't forget diapers, snacks, toys, and anything else that will make their stay comfortable. Resorts with kids' clubs often provide some amenities, but having familiar items from home can make your child feel more at ease.

- **Family-Friendly Swimwear**: Consider swimwear with added sun protection or rash guards for kids, especially if you plan to spend a lot of time at the beach or pool.

- **Travel Games and Entertainment**: For downtime in between excursions, bring a few games, books, or electronic devices to keep the little ones entertained.

No matter your style of travel, packing the right items will ensure you have everything you need to make your trip to Punta Cana enjoyable and stress-free.

Final Thoughts on Embracing Punta Cana's Culture and Natural Beauty

Punta Cana's allure lies not only in its pristine beaches and luxurious resorts but also in its vibrant culture and stunning natural landscapes. Whether you're lounging on white sandy beaches, hiking through lush jungles, or immersing yourself in the warmth of local traditions, Punta Cana has something to offer every type of traveler.

For those looking to embrace the local culture, don't miss the chance to sample authentic Dominican cuisine, shop at bustling markets, or visit small villages to learn about the country's rich heritage. Punta Cana offers an exciting fusion of modern luxury and traditional Dominican experiences, providing a perfect blend of relaxation and adventure.

Equally important is respecting the region's natural beauty. From the crystal-clear waters of the Caribbean to the lush forests and towering mountains, Punta Cana is a paradise that must be preserved. Embrace sustainable travel practices, support eco-friendly businesses, and leave only footprints behind to ensure that future generations can enjoy the same natural wonders.

Preparing for Your Trip: Last-Minute Checklist and Resources

As you prepare for your Punta Cana adventure, a few last-minute steps can help ensure you're fully ready for your trip. Here's a checklist to keep in mind before you set off:

Last-Minute Checklist

- **Check Your Passport**: Ensure your passport is up-to-date and will remain valid for at least six months after your planned departure date.

- **Book Your Excursions**: If there are specific tours or activities you want to do, be sure to book them in advance to avoid disappointment.

- **Confirm Airport Transfers**: Double-check your airport transfer arrangements to ensure a smooth arrival and departure.

- **Pack Health Essentials**: If you take any prescription medications, ensure you have enough for your entire trip. Also, consider bringing a basic first-aid kit with band-aids, pain relievers, and hand sanitizer.

- **Currency and Tips**: While many places in Punta Cana accept credit cards, it's a good idea to carry some local currency (Dominican Pesos) for small purchases or tipping.

Useful Resources

- **Local Websites**: Visit official Dominican Republic tourism websites for up-to-date information on travel advisories, local events, and COVID-19 guidelines.

- **Travel Apps**: Download travel apps such as Google Maps for navigation, and check out local apps for taxi services or restaurant recommendations.

- **Emergency Contacts**: Save emergency numbers, including the local embassy, hotel, and medical services, in case of unforeseen circumstances.

Printed in Dunstable, United Kingdom

70292075R00094